What Happens Next: Messages from Heaven

What Happens Next: Messages from Heaven

A Workbook for Dying and Living

Kay Talbot Ph.D with John Michael

All rights reserved.

No part of this book may be reproduced or stored in a retrieval system, or transmitted in any form or by any means, electronic, mechanical, photocopying, recording, or otherwise, without express written permission of the publisher.

This book is designed to provide information and motivation to our readers. It is sold with the understanding that the publisher is not engaged to render any type of psychological, legal, or any other kind of professional advice. The content of each part and chapter is the sole expression and opinion of its authors, and not necessarily that of the publisher. No warranties or guarantees are expressed or implied by the publisher's choice to include any of the content in this volume.

Neither the publisher nor the individual authors shall be liable for any physical, psychological, emotional, financial, or commercial damages, including, but not limited to, special, incidental, consequential or other damages. Our views and rights are the same: you are responsible for your own choices, actions, and results.

Copyright © 2015 Kay Talbot Ph.D
All rights reserved.

ISBN: 1512282715
ISBN 13: 9781512282719
Library of Congress Control Number: 2015908884
CreateSpace Independent Publishing Platform
North Charleston, South Carolina

"SYMPTOMS OF INNER PEACE tm" by Saskia Davis, Copyright 1984, Saskia Davis LLC. All Rights Reserved. Contact information for reprint permission can be found at www.symptomsofinnerpeace.net

This book is dedicated to our readers: blessings for your journey.

How to Use this Book

Welcome reader! We hope this workbook for living and dying will be both interesting and useful to you.

Our first suggestion is that you not judge the contents you're about to read until you have finished the book. By then you will know what you choose to believe about it. As has been said: "There is a principle which is a bar against all information, which is proof against all arguments, and which cannot fail to keep a (hu)man in everlasting ignorance. That principle is contempt prior to investigation." Rev. William H. Poole (1880-1896).

There are several ways you might use this book. Some will look at the Table of Contents and select a starting point, perhaps a message from someone famous. Others will read through to the end without answering any of the questions included, saving them for another time. Still others will start at the beginning and proceed slowly, using the contemplation questions to reflect on and then answering them. Thus, there is no one best way to go through the workbook; there is only your way. Begin by turning to the Introduction for more information.

Table of Contents

HOW TO USE THIS BOOK ·vii
INTRODUCTION · xi

PART ONE: THOSE UNPREPARED TO DIE · · · · · · · · · · · 1
  An Unfinished Song · 1
  Playful Spirit · 7
  Father Abraham Returns· 12
  Justice Warrior · 17
  Both Sides Now · 22
  Band of Brothers· 28
  Shot in the Back · 34

PART TWO: PEOPLE SOMEWHAT PREPARED TO DIE · · 41
  My Young Friend · 41
  Much Better Now · 47
  Gone Too Soon · 53
  Beloved Clown · 60
  The Good Wife· 66
  Both Human and Spiritual · 72
  More Life Next · 78

PART THREE: PEOPLE PREPARED TO DIE · · · · · · · · · · · 85
   The Good Nurse · 85
   Light for Living · 92
   Dying Doctor · 98
   Change of Direction · 103
   Dying Like A Saint · 108
   Long Life Writer · 115
   His Plan Fulfilled · 122

PART FOUR: CONCLUSION · 129
   Summary and Acknowledgements · · · · · · · · · · · · · 129
   Guided Meditation ·132
   The Impact of Spiritual Beliefs During
   Times of Personal Crisis · 134
   References ·137
   Annotated Bibliography ·139
   About the Authors ·149

Introduction

This workbook tells the story of people who have moved beyond this life in the body to living in the spirit. Each of us will get to experience this movement at some point in our lives. This dying is a process that starts today and ends when our spirit moves beyond the body into spiritual living. Some of us will go joyfully into our next life. Some of us face that time fearfully. Each of us will experience this journey from life in the body into a life that will be radically new to us in spirit.

This is not the book we thought we would write. It is the book that the Great Spirit, which we choose to call God, helped us write. It is a series of stories and messages from people who have died and our responses to those messages. Not all will believe these spirit messages, but we ask you to suspend judgment until you have read the book. Take from it what is helpful to you at this time in your life.

After meditating, John invited the spirit of a young woman who had died recently to show him ways to help her mother with her grief. Surprisingly, the spirit of Abby came forward and did just that, as John wrote her responses down. Later, John called upon the spirits of certain famous people and individual patients he had worked with as a hospital chaplain to respond to his questions. As he says, he held the pen but the answers that followed did not come from him. They did not go through his brain; and a lot of the information they offered was unknown to him at that time. He was merely the spirit scribe.

Kay read each written dialogue, contemplated it, and has provided guiding questions for you, the reader. Your answers to these questions will make this your own personal workbook and plan for your life now and during your final days on Earth. Our hope is that this will be a comforting, and yes, sometimes, a challenging book but one that you can use in your own unique way. Some will write their thoughts and prayers; others will draw as well; and some will include photos and pictures representing important people, events, feelings, or ideas. The messages and questions included here have the potential to change your life. At the least they will often provide a different perspective for looking at the decisions we make as we live and ultimately die.

So this is a spiritual workbook, the stories of 21 people who have experienced dying. Their spirits tell us about their process of dying and how it is for them now. The workbook includes ways readers can prepare for the life of the spirit. For all important trips we take, we need to plan wisely if they are to be meaningful to us and peaceful. We hope this workbook will help you plan for your living and dying. May each minute of your preparation for your unique journey be sacred.

The workbook is organized by messages at the beginning from people who died suddenly and were not prepared to die, then from those who were somewhat prepared, followed by those who were well prepared to die. Some were obviously famous people while on Earth; others were everyday people whose spirits came to share their wisdom with us.

While this is a spiritual workbook, it is not intended to be used to convert people in any religious way. Rather, we hope to bring you closer to the God of your understanding. We believe that people of all religions will be able to benefit from using this workbook. As we release this work for publication, we pray for you, our readers, and wish you a joyful life and a peaceful transition at the end. Perhaps we shall meet on the other side, which we and many others call home.

Part One: Those Unprepared to Die

Part one presents the dying stories of those who did not expect death. Five of the seven had lived a public life. Some issues had been addressed but these people were not prepared for the specifics of the dying process.

The first chapter presents the story of a young woman who died while on Spring break in her first year of college. Her death was sudden, unexpected, and attracted the attention of thousands in its mysterious way. Abby was beloved by many, admired greatly, and is missed by all those who wonder at her passing. Abby was the first to tell her story from the other side.

An Unfinished Song

ABBY, WOULDN'T YOU SAY THAT YOU HAD AN INTERESTING LIFE?
It was rather short. It was sort of an unfinished song. That is why I am working through you and others in this world so that I can have a full song to present. I am a work in progress. I am anxious to have a finished song to present.

WHO WOULD YOU PRESENT THIS FINISHED SONG TO?
There is a gatekeeper of sorts at the gate to the next level. Either you stay in this level or you get to pass on to the next level. I am working on my song completion.

I GO BACK AGAIN TO THE QUESTION OF YOUR DYING. WERE YOU TAKEN EARLY FOR A REASON?
Yes. The fact that I was taken early comes from someone else. I did not actively want to die. I wanted something else, so dying came as much as a surprise to me as it did to everyone else.

DO YOU KNOW WHO TOOK YOU AND WHY?
Here is the main question. I am still finding out the meaning in all of this. I believe that it was God who took me out of life for a better reason. I don't know all about what that reason is, but it has to do with God's will and glory. It is for the glory of God. We all have to learn and find out what purpose all this served. I know that I am happier in this better place, but I don't know the whole story. God does not send text messages here either.

WHAT HELPS YOU FROM MY LIVING?
Open; open; open. You are an open channel for the most part. Most people have a set of rules that work in the human world, but not in the life of the spirit. You are so open that I can work through you and experiment with you. You don't judge or go off. I do some funny things just to experiment and learn.

WHAT HELPS ME FROM YOUR LIVING?
You feel inspired by my energy. I let you know things that allow you to not get down about the limitation of the human world. You and I know your history of being disappointed about parts of life. I work to short circuit that before it takes over. You must know that you are less disappointed than before.

Part One: Those Unprepared to Die

WHAT HAVE YOU LEARNED IN SPIRIT?

The easy answer is so much. It is more challenging for us to be specific as I am in spirit and you are human. You are open to what I send you now. I love more fully now. Humans have so many reasons to hold back love. There is no good reason – just love. You pray and say Alleluia. I suggest that you do that from your heart and soul. Say my name and say Alleluia from your heart and spirit, less from your head. The heart word is like a direct current in the universe. The head word is like alternating current – off and on; yes and no; one and zero. Keep it direct.

CONTEMPLATION (Abby)
Even though Abby says she is "happier" in "this better place", she also points out how surprised she was at her own death. She works to complete her "unfinished song" by bringing light and energy to others. When someone dies unexpectedly and of unknown causes, loved ones are left to make sense of such a shocking tragedy. Their lives go from sunlit color to shades of grey the instant they hear the news. It takes time to realize what has happened and what it means.

By all accounts Abby was loved and admired by a great number of people. As an organ donor she has brought new life to many waiting for such a precious gift. Is this something you would like to have happen if possible when you die? Completing your State's organ donation form will help assure this.

After the funeral or memorial, survivors confront the question: what can we do now that is meaningful? Ensuring the loved one is never forgotten is important and can take many different forms. Some of these are creating a memorial album that can serve as a biography; writing songs or poems or prayers; taking part in a yearly tribute that remembers what the loved one was like. As the first chapter of this workbook Abby's story invites you into the dialogue about sudden, unexpected death. If this were to happen to you, in what ways would you want to be remembered by those you leave behind?

_____
_____
_____
_____
_____

Part One: Those Unprepared to Die

Do you find it comforting that Abby is able to continue working on her song on the other side? Can you describe or draw a picture of what the other side means to you at this point in your life?

_____
_____
_____
_____
_____

The morning glory blooms but for an hour
And yet it differs not at heart
From the giant pine
That lives for a thousand years.
Teitoku Matsunaga, 16th century Japanese poet

Playful Spirit

At the age of nine, Lily died suddenly and unexpectedly from a brain seizure, leaving those who loved her in shock and deep grief. She returns to encourage all humans to learn their lessons and then to move on to find joy in life before slipping into spirit.

I INVITE LILY TO BRING HER MESSAGE. WHAT DO YOU HAVE TO SHARE?
It has been a long time for me to wait to tell my story. I love telling stories and making people happy. I do that a lot here. We entertain each other with our stories and adventures. I wish humans could see life more as an adventure and less like a chore. I travel. I talk. I work at play for the benefit of others.

IT SOUNDS LIKE YOU ENJOY YOUR LIFE.
Yes. Living in spirit is not that much different from being alive as a human. The big difference is that this body is purer than the earth body. Your body is made up of elements that are part of the earth. Our bodies are lighter. They "fit" better to who we really are. You take on bodies to experience what you have to go through during your human lives. My body as little Lily was challenging for me. I learned through body experiences that were needed for me. Now I have a lighter body.

DO YOU HAVE ANY MESSAGES FOR US?
Yes. Free up your ways of living. Humans stay in their own prisons too long. You are human to go through something, but not to stay in something. Keep moving through what you have to learn there. Do not make a long term prison sentence of that which is meant to be a short stay. Most

of human suffering is from human causes. Learn the lesson and then move on. You would say, let go and let God. Personally humans do better when they take the course, complete the class, graduate, and then move on.

IS THAT WHAT YOU DID?
Yes. My human life was short because I just had a limited lesson to learn. I needed to learn a simple lesson and then let go of that human body so that I could take on this light body. My lesson was easier to learn in a human body and then let it go and go to spirit and God. Tell people not to cling to their bodies too long.

IT IS EASY TO WRITE IN THIS PLACE. WHY?
I come here often to visit my mom and check in on her. I motivate her to travel and get active with new things. She would do well to get more active. But for now I can visit here and slide into her. I focus on her energy form wherever she is, but she is easier to reach here, so I am used to checking into this place for communicating. Write here often in the early morning. I can easily share more. But most of all, encourage my mom and everyone to enjoy their lives and learn their lessons before they go into spirit.

Part One: Those Unprepared to Die

CONTEMPLATION (Lily)
Lily encourages us to see life as an adventure. When have you ventured forth in search of excitement, new experiences, challenging activities, new places, and/or new people to meet? What was the result of your taking the risk to embrace something new?

_____
_____
_____

She also encourages us to share our stories with others and take time to play. When was the last time you sat down to talk with someone and tell stories? When have you stopped working and let yourself just play? Write down examples.

_____
_____
_____

When we learn lessons in life, Lily advises us to take them in and then to move on to the next adventure. What lesson have you learned lately?

_____
_____
_____

The result of spontaneous adventure and play is often laughter and inner peace. Read the following list of symptoms of inner peace every day for a week. At the end of the week, do you find yourself living out some of these symptoms? If not, keep reading the list each day and work to "let go and let God". Describe your progress and identify anything that is holding you back from approaching life as an adventure.

___

<u>Signs and Symptoms of Inner Peace</u> By Saskia Davis copyright 1984. All rights reserved.

A tendency to think and act spontaneously rather than on fears based on past experiences.
An unmistakable ability to enjoy each moment.
A loss of interest in judging other people.
A loss of interest in judging self.
A loss of interest in interpreting the actions of others.
A loss of interest in conflict.
A loss of ability to worry.
Frequent, overwhelming episodes of appreciation.
Contented feelings of connectedness with others and nature.
Frequent attacks of smiling.
An increasing tendency to let things happen rather than make them happen.
An increased susceptibility to love extended by others and the uncontrollable urge to extend it.

___

My inventory of inner peace:

Father Abraham Returns

What President is more beloved than Abraham Lincoln? Who was better fitted to lead this young nation? Who still watches over this country from his mighty throne?

I INVITE IN THE SPIRIT OF ABRAHAM LINCOLN. HOW WAS YOUR DYING PROCESS?

My dying process was well documented from the point of view of the shot to the back of my head in the theater. The untold story was what happened over the next hours and my journey into spirit. Because we are just getting to know each other, I will keep this brief for now. Some of my best decisions and speeches were brief and simple.

BECAUSE WE ARE JUST GETTING TO KNOW EACH OTHER, I WILL JUST ASK FOR THE SIMPLE THINGS. WHAT DO YOU WANT TO SHARE?

The simple truth--I was shot. I did not know it was coming consciously but I had a sense of foreboding. I deeply resented resistance of the enemy in moving forward for what was best for this nation. I held these feelings and thoughts. They came to be that pain in my head. I could have been more open about my experience. I did not surround myself with like-minded people. My advisors and my family were oppositional. That was what I was accustomed to in my early life. I went into books and the law to deal with opposition. Today the heads of state surround themselves with loyal aides and a family that is supportive. When I was president we were at war with each other. For the most part I was a war president. When I was alive, winning the internal war in the country was most important.

Part One: Those Unprepared to Die

FROM YOUR LIFE IN SPIRIT, WHAT IS THE STORY THAT YOU WANT TO TELL?
I would like to tell the story of the better angels of our lives. Here in spirit it is easier to live out the better ways. In your human world, there is a mix of influences. It is complex for humans. Here I see the thing as it is. I see the people as they are. I see the idea in a fresh light.

WHAT ADVICE WOULD YOU SHARE WITH US?
Move the complex toward the simple. Short speeches are better than long speeches. Small words are better than big words. Short prayers are better than long prayers. Keep it simple humanly and spiritually. That is my deepest joy now -- the simple contemplation of the universe. Universe – "one word" in Latin; all is one.

DO OUR BEST WISHES REACH YOU?
Yes. People need simple images. I love the memorial to me in Washington, the Capital. People come every day with a cavalcade of thoughts, prayers, tears, and various emotions. I check in every day there. That place is so full of a daily outpouring. You have liked it there; go back again – back in the grace of that place. It is the living legacy of all that I wanted to do for this nation. It is there that I am paid back for that hard life that I lived so long ago as Abraham Lincoln, father of a new nation with liberty and justice for all.

THANK YOU.

CONTEMPLATION (Abraham Lincoln)
Abraham Lincoln is today one of our most revered and deeply respected presidents. He was assassinated on April 14, 1865 by John Wilkes Booth, who resented the president's stand against slavery. The country was divided over the issue of slavery and the Civil War began after seven southern States seceded. In your own life, who do you revere and why?

_____
_____
_____
_____
_____

What beliefs do you hold strongly and are willing to work to uphold?

_____
_____
_____
_____
_____

On April 15, 2015 church bells rang out at the Lincoln Memorial in Washington, DC to mark 150 years since Lincoln's assassination. Lincoln calls the Memorial a place of grace and "the living legacy of all I wanted to do for this nation". The word grace comes from the Greek "charis" and stands for the kindness bestowed by God on all, including those who do not seem to deserve it. Grace is recognized by many organized religions and is frequently accompanied by the term mercy. In your life thus far can you remember

Part One: Those Unprepared to Die

times when you acted with kindness and mercy? --when you felt God's grace?

_____
_____
_____
_____
_____

Lincoln also notes that his best decisions and speeches were simple and brief. He advises us to try to live our lives this way as well. Read "The Impact of Spiritual Beliefs during Times of Personal Crisis" in Part Four. How would you describe your spiritual beliefs at this point in your life?

_____
_____
_____
_____
_____

> **"In this temple as in the hearts of the people for whom he saved the union the memory of Abraham Lincoln is enshrined forever."**
>
> — INSCRIBED ON THE LINCOLN MEMORIAL, WASHINGTON, D.C.

Justice Warrior

Dr. Martin Luther King, Jr. was a warrior for justice who had the courage to give his life for us. The martyr's crown did not frighten him. What great glory in laying down one's life for the good of all.

I INVITE IN THE SPIRIT OF MARTIN LUTHER KING JR. DR. KING WHAT DO YOU HAVE TO SHARE?
I am glad to see that you have Christ with you. That is the central source for living this life in this world. You have seen much in this life and this is the central way of living life well. I am glad that you will be here this day for the vigil of the mystery of the Passion of Christ. It is a mystery that can be thought about and experienced, but never fully understood. Remember, don't try to know or understand, but have the wisdom to appreciate the truth as it is.

THANK YOU. WHAT WAS YOUR DYING LIKE?
It was sudden. I was standing and talking and the next thing I knew I was lying down with people around me looking worried. Then I was floating above the scene with the certainty that I was in spirit and dead to the world. It had been made known to me that I would not live long. I believe that God let it happen for a reason.

DO YOU BELIEVE THAT YOU WERE TAKEN BY GOD?
Yes. I have learned that God works in mysterious ways for his glory to be known. I was of more glory to God as a martyr than as a speaker for just causes. More grace would flow through my being martyred in the South than all the prizes and awards would ever bring to the betterment of the people and the races. God was wise in taking my life.

COULD YOU SAY MORE ABOUT THAT?
There is a way that God works in the world that defies human logic and fulfills spiritual truth. You often quote the scripture that God's thoughts are not man's thoughts, and that human ways are not God's ways. Exactly. There is no more effective way to bring justice than the effect of an unjust murder. The murder of Jesus; the murder of Lincoln; and the murder of Kennedy were all moves toward bringing justice into our unfair world. The cost may be great, but the effect was also great.

Jesus was able to move through the Roman Empire as a result of his being murdered. His murder was made glorious in the lives of oppressed people. The sacrifice for the greater good is the principle that is at work in these instances. The murder of a good man has great effect in the lives of many.

I was aware that I would not have a long life and agreed on some level. Lincoln, Kennedy, we all knew at some level about the nature of our sacrifice for the greater good. We may not have thought about it daily, but we knew that we were heading for the martyr's crown and agreed to that way of dying. What greater love than to lie down one's life for the well-being of the greater good?

Part One: Those Unprepared to Die

CONTEMPLATION (Martin Luther King Jr.)
Imagine the courage it takes to know you are going to be killed for your beliefs and to act on those beliefs anyway. Read these excerpts from Dr. King's 1963 speech at the Lincoln Memorial in Washington, D.C.:

"Now is the time to make real the promises of democracy. Now is the time to rise from the dark and desolate valley of segregation to the sunlit path of racial justice. Now is the time to lift our nation from the quicksand of racial injustice to the solid rock of brotherhood. Now is the time to make justice a reality for all of God's children.

... In the process of gaining our rightful place, we must not be guilty of wrongful deeds. Let us not seek to satisfy our thirst for freedom by drinking from the cup of bitterness and hatred. We must forever conduct our struggle on the high plane of dignity and discipline. We must not allow our creative protest to degenerate into physical violence. Again and again, we must rise to the majestic heights of meeting physical force with soul force.

... I have a dream that my four little children will one day live in a nation where they will not be judged by the color of their skin but by the content of their character."

Do you believe Dr. King's dream continues to play out on the streets of our country? Has our Nation made progress toward bringing justice to an unfair world? What ways would you use to measure a complete end to racism in this country?

_____
_____
_____
_____
_____

What actions have you taken so far in your life that took courage despite any fear you felt?

_____
_____
_____
_____
_____

How did you feel after taking courageous action?

_____
_____
_____
_____
_____

> **"Courage is being scared to death – and saddling up anyway."**
>
> — JOHN WAYNE, ACTOR

Both Sides Now

For many Americans, the death of President Kennedy was the most dramatic event of their lives. It is amazing to think that he still walks the halls of the White House; he now sees both sides of life.

I INVITE THE SPIRIT OF JOHN KENNEDY IN NOW. WHAT WAS YOUR DYING LIKE?
I was shocked by the suddenness of the death scene. I was not unfamiliar with death and the subject of dying. I had read much. The tragedy of the day was so unexpected. I was feeling lively and confident and the next thing I knew I was grabbing my throat because of the pain. Then I was immediately outside my body looking down at the chaos. I stayed with my body because that was what I knew.

THE QUESTION THAT HANGS IN HISTORY IS: WHO KILLED KENNEDY?" WHO DID?
The shot that killed me came from an angry man in front of me --back and to the left. That bullet drove my body back. I was not in my body at that time. With the first shot I was out of my body watching. Spiritually, I knew to get out of my body quickly. I saw the bullet slam into my head and drive it backwards.

SO THAT IS WHO PULLED THE TRIGGER. DO YOU WANT TO ADD ANYTHING ELSE?
I did not know how hated I was by so many powerful men. I did not know the extent of the plotting to assassinate me as leader of the country. I was naïve from my present point of view. In retrospect, I could have been more mindful of how to be protected. We did not know then the degree of malevolence that was afoot in the world. I could have been more aware of how to prevent evil as I tried to do good.

Part One: Those Unprepared to Die

WHAT HAPPENED TO YOU JUST AFTER THE DYING SCENE?
I was met by family, friends, angels, and saints and spirits of many kinds. I was uplifted immediately by the well-wishes and prayers of the world. I was so elated by the experience that it took me awhile to start to understand what had happened. There was so much energy and grace for me that I felt elated. Only in retrospect did I fathom the enormity of what had happened.

WHAT HAVE YOU LEARNED OVER THESE FIFTY YEARS?
We don't count years here. It is all spirit and light. I have been curious to learn what that was all about. People have a certain idea about me, but I was not like Joe or Bobby. I was the more serious, introspective one. I have been studying the records to learn and help the process of power. I still visit the White House and walk the halls I loved to walk. You cannot imagine what it is like to live as the head of state. I work to help present presidents. It is both a burden and a glory to live through that role.

WHAT NOW?
My life review was unique because of all the love and prayer that came to me. Many still pray. It is very moving and I am very appreciative. I appreciate your prayers for Jacqueline. She is better now. Pray for all of us who are in spirit and on the sidelines. You are on the field; we are watching.

WOULD YOU WANT TO ADD MORE FOR US?
Encourage everyone to put more effort into their spiritual lives as they live their human lives. Just as athletes train for their events, train for the process of dying. It does not happen just in a moment if it is done well. Dying takes place over a period of time and preparation takes place over a

period of time. Talking is good; writing is better. Writing is good; praying is better. Praying is good; meditation is better. All efforts toward dying with a purpose are helpful. Just as each person has their own life plan, each person has a plan for dying that is right for them.

I had not started my training for dying when my life was ended. If you have time to prepare, put effort and work into your dying. My dying was tragic for many reasons. One of the reasons is that I did not get to fulfill my dying for the purpose that God had in store for me. If I had lived, I could have been a great teacher and counselor for many. Just as my speeches were meant to be tools for teaching, I could have taught leaders and students of many kinds. That is what I am doing in spirit – using my podium to teach and lead others in spirit. **THANK YOU.**

Part One: Those Unprepared to Die

CONTEMPLATION (John Kennedy)
Those of us who were alive fifty years ago remember just where we were when we heard the president had been assassinated. It was as if the world stood still. He was our 35th and youngest president, born to wealth and privilege yet dedicated to work to improve the country. In shock and pain he left his body and looked down at the chaos below. He says he was naïve and didn't realize how hated he was by so many powerful men. One life was taken but the enormity of losing the country's leader continued as people tried to take in what happened. When have you been shocked by the evil in our world?

_____
_____
_____

Do you offer prayers for the victims? What is it like for you to be told that such prayers bring their spirits energy and grace?

_____
_____
_____

Do you believe the spirits of the departed carry on to help those left behind? In the White House there is still much to learn about the process of power. It is an awesome responsibility to be president of this country. If you could tell our president one uplifting thing, what would it be?

_____
_____
_____

Feeling capable, skillful, qualified, strong, assured, and influential are all words for feeling powerful. In your own life, when have you felt <u>powerful</u>?

_____
_____
_____

When have you felt <u>powerless</u>?

_____
_____
_____

Death can make us feel powerless and murder even more so. We have one choice and that is how we react to death. We can decide to always remember our loved ones who die before us. JFK left us these words, among others:

> **"And so, my fellow Americans: ask not what your country can do for you – ask what you can do for your country. My fellow citizens of the world: ask not what America will do for you, but what together we can do for the freedom of man."**
>
> –JOHN F. KENNEDY, INAUGURAL ADDRESS, JANUARY 20, 1961

What words would you like to leave behind for loved ones after your death?

_____
_____
_____

Band of Brothers

Robert Kennedy speaks clearly about both following the plan for his life and getting off the path. He speaks of the glory of the Kennedy family and the unfulfilled promise of his family.

I INVITE IN THE SPIRIT OF ROBERT KENNEDY. HOW WAS YOUR DYING?
I had much the same experience as my brother. I was shot by an angry man who used a gun to express his anger. I was able to jump out of my body before the head shot. I viewed my dying from above. There was chaos and mayhem for a period of time. I knew that my body was dead and it took some time for the body systems to lose energy and stop working. That takes a while naturally. I was long out of my body by the time that physical death occurred.

WITH ALL DUE RESPECT, YOU SOUND DIFFERENT FROM YOUR BROTHER JOHN.
We are different kinds of spirits and were different kinds of people. He was more charismatic. I was more interested in how things worked. He was head of state, and I was attorney general. Those roles fit our priorities. Being president was not really my best way of being of help and fulfilling our destiny.

WHAT DO YOU MEAN BY "OUR DESTINY"?
Yes, we came here at a time when the life of this world was going to change dramatically. We, the four of us, came here with an agenda to brighten this world and act as leaders. That was the plan. We came here as a band of brothers to innovate and lead. Obviously, it did not all work out, but some of it did work. All Americans and many around the world are freer as a result of our efforts.

Part One: Those Unprepared to Die

WHAT HAVE YOU LEARNED IN SPIRIT?
Follow the plan. God has a plan and the unfolding of that plan depends on how humans live out that plan. We Kennedys acted out part of the plan but not all of it; we could have been more diligent. We could have avoided the pitfalls.

IN RETROSPECT, WHAT COULD HAVE BEEN BETTER?
There are so many lessons to learn in spirit. You live a life and learn more about it in spirit. Personally, I could have been more dedicated to my role as who I was. I was not Joe. I was not John. I was the underdog, the runt of the litter. I tried too hard. You would say, let the game come to you. I would now say, travel the path with heart. In religion I was too much like Calvin. In government, I was too much like Napoleon. Let the plan unfold as it is meant to unfold. I forced the issue too much. We didn't stick to the greater plan enough. It could have been better. We three did not have to get killed in the process.

WOW! CAN YOU SAY MORE?
Much more. Naturally in spirit I went looking for the reasons and influences that worked against our living completely full lives. I underestimated the forces of our enemy. I would live differently if I knew then the ways of the enemy kingdom. Their ways are dark and twisted and hard to decipher. It is a shadow world that stalks the light world. They are always there, lurking in the shadows and the back kitchens.

IS THAT A REFERENCE TO WHERE YOU WERE SHOT?
Yes -- obviously. It was ignorant to be on my way to Chicago and yet I was so unprotected against the gunman in the shadows of that basement kitchen. They lurk and

lurk, watching for their ambush times. Be careful; beware of darkness. Stay in the light.

I CAN'T HELP BUT ASK ABOUT THE PERSON NAMED MARILYN MONROE IN THIS STORY.
That poor girl. She was so tormented and so used. It is such a source of evil and darkness that they use the weak and turn them into fools. Drugs are the main way to use humans today, but many devices are used to bring down humans. That particular human was brought down and used in a deplorable way. The story is obvious. It did no good for our family. Prayer and healing and forgiveness come first.

SPEAKING OF PRAYER, WHAT DO YOU WANT TO SHARE ABOUT THAT?
Prayer and sacrifice go a long way toward bringing light into the darkness. The plan is always designed for good. Grace is needed to bring that plan to fruition. Travel with the light.

THANK YOU.
It's my pleasure. Let's do this again.

Part One: Those Unprepared to Die

CONTEMPLATION (Robert Kennedy)
Yet another assassination! This time, on June 5, 1968 it was the Attorney General of the United States, Robert Kennedy. He says God had a plan to use him, and his brothers, to help brighten the world. They worked to make Americans and others around the world freer. Like his brother JFK, he says he underestimated the forces that worked against him. As a result of his murder, all candidates for president are now provided secret service protection.

Our world continues to confront evil; RFK says that prayer and sacrifice "go a long way toward bringing light into the darkness." Perhaps he means that we need to pray that God will soften the hearts of those who do evil. That is certainly the message that Jesus brought – to turn our thoughts away from revenge and toward reconciliation. If you have ever prayed for a personal enemy to have goodness in their life, then you know this is very difficult to do. Do it anyway. Do it often. Notice how over time you begin to think less about that person and more about what is good in your life. It will be as though his or her power has been diminished and eventually their power over you will have melted away. Notice that you no longer wish for revenge or carry around resentment. What force of darkness do you need to pray for today?

_____
_____
_____

God's plans are "always designed for good," we are told, and we are to travel in the light of that goodness. Do you have a plan for your life that includes doing good and bringing light to those around you? Perhaps you do some volunteer work, donate money to a good cause, and vote for laws aimed at social justice.

_____
_____
_____

In the year 2000 movie <u>Pay It Forward</u> (Kevin Spacey & Helen Hunt), a young boy develops his own plan to bring light to the world. Borrow, rent, or buy the movie and see how that works. The message is simple: "Do not be overcome by evil, but overcome evil with good". (Romans 12:21). A simple prayer at the start of your day can make all the difference: "God, make me a blessing to someone today."

> **"Let no one be discouraged by the belief that there is nothing one person can do against the enormous array of the world's illness, misery, ignorance and violence. Few have the greatness to bend history, but each of us can work to change a small portion of events. And in the total of all those acts will be written the history of a generation."**
>
> — ROBERT KENNEDY

Shot in the Back
This next account is of a person who was shot in the back while in the full bloom of life. His life was lived fully but he did not have the benefit of preparing for the actual event of dying. This is the story of rock star John Lennon.

JOHN, I OFTEN TELL PEOPLE THAT YOU ARE MY HERO.
Well isn't that just nice. I am just another person who said what he felt. A lot of good it did.

MANY OF US THINK IT DID A LOT OF GOOD. BUT STAYING ON TARGET: HOW WAS YOUR DYING?
I am going to hope that is not a bad pun. I was the target for him and for many. I was shot in a way that I did not expect. It was late and I was tired so I signed the autograph and walked on. Then I was feeling pain all over and falling to the ground. I came around in the hospital with all the people buzzing around my body. I pretty much knew that I was dead.

WHAT WAS THAT LIKE FOR YOU?
It was really a relief. Life for me was not a walk in the park. Every day was a new challenge. I felt like I had to challenge the world. That was the way that life was set up. I had to challenge the world, to change the world. Being off the merry-go-round was a relief.

HOW IS LIFE FOR YOU NOW?
I see much more now. I always was into something new. That was a name I put to an early album – check it out. Now, so much is new. I see life more like it is. Life is really simple. Human life is more complex because of the many influences on us there. Here we are in our real place. It took me awhile

Part One: Those Unprepared to Die

to get here because I had to detox from all that before I got to be with my kindred spirits. It is where those like me come from.

CAN YOU TALK ABOUT YOUR KINDRED SPIRITS?
I don't know anyone here that I knew there. These spirits are easier for me to be with. We are as we are. Human people mostly want something. I never met a person who did not want something. I never met a human who just wanted to be with me. If I had known one, that life would have been different.

DO YOU WANT TO TALK ABOUT YOUR LIFE?
Well, yes and no. My life review was very extensive. So much happened in that life; I may have to go back. That is not up to me.

WHO IS IT UP TO?
You may want me to say God. It is a greater power from above. I am still learning about that greater power. I believe in me. Only being a parent changed that; I still work on being me mostly. It is easier and simpler here to do that.

DO YOU HAVE ANY ADVICE FROM SPIRIT FOR HUMANS?
Of course, that is the question. How can I give advice from here? You are open to me now. What is it that you are feeling?

I FEEL GRATEFUL THAT I CAN HAVE THIS EXPERIENCE WITH YOU.
You feel grateful for the messages. You still sing those songs to yourself sometimes. It is not me; it is the music. You said that after doing this (receiving messages from spirit), you

are in an altered state. I was in an altered state doing music. My advice would be to open up and let spirit flow through you. That is what I did with the music. That is what you do with meditation. It happens every day. No plans. Just let the higher spirit flow through you.

DO YOU WANT TO EXPRESS ANYTHING ELSE NOW?
Encourage humans to get into spirit before their bodies die. We never know about tomorrow. Today each human can get into spirit. Life is more than the body. If you are ready before dying, the transition goes so much better. I was sort of ready, but not really. My mind knew it was going to stop being, but my spirit was not ready to move toward home. Thus the long transition period I had to get here.

CAN WE WHO ARE GRATEFUL HELP YOU?
Certainly; I get messages of caring and love still. That has not changed. I feel encouraged when I get messages. It is like when you humans get flowers. We get messages that are like flowers to us here in spirit. I like it best when I get a message that says that something I said helps someone there today. It is the combination of love and gratitude that moves me most.

Part One: Those Unprepared to Die

CONTEMPLATION (John Lennon)
John Lennon speaks to us from the place he calls home. Surprisingly, his dying brought him relief. HIs rock star life on the world stage brought constant challenges. Now he no longer feels he must change the world. His life was complex, relentlessly changing, and frequently not in his control. As he sang in an album (Double Fantasy): "Life is what happens to you while you're busy making other plans." So much happened in his life that he regrets; he says he may have to come back. He speaks of a spiritual cleansing that was necessary to allow him to meet his kindred spirits on the other side, which he calls "our real place". If you died suddenly, without preparation and goodbyes to those you love, are there things in your life you might have to come back to rectify? Write them down.

_____
_____
_____

If you have regrets about some things you have done and can't take back, can you think of positive actions you could take to make amends, to add good works that nurture the world? Make a list and start doing them today.

_____
_____
_____

For Lennon music was comforting and led him to "an altered state." What music comforts you; brings happy feelings; gives you energy; touches your heart? Make a list of the music you would like to have around you when you are dying. Start listening to that music now and notice how it affects your spirit.

_____
_____
_____

On the other side, we learn we can be our real selves, and we spend time with new kindred spirits who--unlike people on Earth-- don't want anything from us. Consider this: People feel honored and cared for when we listen to them without talking about ourselves, but with a real interest in finding out who they really are; what they are thinking and feeling. Eye contact and a relaxed atmosphere are essential for this. Take time in your hectic day to listen to someone this way. Write about the response you get and how you feel about this.

_____
_____
_____

"We are not human beings having a spiritual experience but spiritual beings having a human experience."

— Pierre Teilhard de Chardin, Jesuit priest, 1881-1955

Part Two: People Somewhat Prepared to Die

In this second part we read about people who were somewhat prepared to die. They each have unique stories to tell us about their process of dying and their entry into spirit. They were not suddenly shot; they had some knowledge that they were in their final phase of life. They were prepared in some ways for the awesome event of dying.

My Young Friend

I INVITE BILL IN THIS MORNING. BILL, HOW WAS YOUR DYING PROCESS?
You saw me when I was quite active still. I was able to talk and move. I was in pain, but I was conscious. At the end I was not conscious. I had no memories of the last few days until I came to looking at my body. My wife, son, friends, and family were there. I could not communicate with them. That was so frustrating. I was there and they acted like I was not there. I wanted to shout out loud to them, but could not. They were sad and I was frustrated.

DO YOU WANT TO SHARE ANYTHING ELSE?
The prayers of the people were very helpful. Your prayers were helpful. What was not helpful was the fear and sadness of my family. They did not understand that I was going

to be alright. Most of their fuss was about themselves more than for me. I had faith that I was going to be ok. They were so distressed and I could not comfort them. My son was so young that he didn't know the facts, but he could feel the pain of his mother and grandparents. I wish they had the faith that I had.

HOW DID YOUR FAITH AFFECT DYING?
When the worry would come up, I would think about the promises of the Bible and pray. It eased my mind. I did not have to worry and fuss when my faith was strong.

DID YOUR DYING YOUNG HAVE MEANING?
Dying is God's way. From here I can see that there was a plan and a way that God had for my life. I did not understand it when I was human and in a body, but even then God would have his way. Looking back, I wish I had not gone through all the painful treatments. I was going to die anyway. Why go through all the painful treatments? I didn't know. I hoped there was a chance of me having a long life, but that was not God's plan.

DO YOU KNOW WHAT GOD'S PLAN WAS?
Yes. In life review I saw that God had a short life planned for me. I did not know that and started a family and looked at how the world lives rather than God's plan for me. I can see now that my becoming Catholic and being religious was my way of beginning to understand that spiritual things were more important. I did not know that early in life, and lived like the people around me. When it came time for my number to be called, I began to turn toward spiritual things.

FASCINATING BILL!
Yes, it is. There is much that humans do not see. Humans see the surface. There is no comparison to people in spirit. Humans are just children playing.

BILL, I TRAVELLED A LITTLE OF THE JOURNEY WITH YOU
You were fine. You were very faithful. I knew you would be there when you said you would. You prayed for me religiously. That helped in the dying process. Even though I was full of cancer, I did not suffer that much. Prayers help that way. You could be more optimistic with dying people. Carry the light that it will be better. This pain is only temporary. Tell people and hold out that strong hope that people are going to a better place.

BILL, DO WE HAVE ANY FUTURE?
Sure, pray for me and I will pray for you. We get prayers as messages in spirit. Keep on with this hopeful message to people that we live on. Encourage people to prepare better. This is definitely a better place. Tell people that. Hold out that hope. People don't know. Now you know. Tell them about this greater life after dying. Thanks John for the good work. Keep it up. We appreciate it!

CONTEMPLATION (Bill)
Bill's spirit comes to us with purpose – to assure us that we continue in a greater life after dying.

As he looks back on his dying process, he remembers some of the emotions he felt. He felt frustration at not being able to let his family know that he was right there with them as they viewed his body. Is he telling us that the desire to be in control can stay with us even after we pass on – at least at the beginning?

Bill talks of a regret he has – the decision to undergo painful cancer treatments with the hope that they might allow him more time here. What decisions do you face at this time or are likely to face in the future? Write them down. Pray for God's guidance as you begin to face them.

_____
_____
_____

Ultimately Bill decides that God has had a plan for his life all along and that his family members have their own lives to lead. He no longer wishes to try to control their grief.

If you left your body today, what emotions might you take with you? What emotions could you decide to resolve while you're still here? Naming our emotions is actually a way of beginning to acknowledge them and the start of letting them go. Separating our emotions from those of others is a way of owning <u>our</u> current reality, not theirs. Prayer is a powerful way to let negative emotions go. What are you called to pray for today?

_____
_____
_____

Part Two: People Somewhat Prepared to Die

As we give to God the thoughts and feelings that are causing us psychic pain, we become freer to share memories, love, and joy with people we choose to be with us during our dying. We can choose who we want around us. Who would you want to be with you during this time? Can you let them know what would be helpful to you and what wouldn't? Can you say: "thank you for...; I forgive you for...; I'm sorry about...; goodbye; and may God bless you.

_____
_____
_____

Those who hope in the Lord will renew their strength.
   They will soar on wings like eagles; they will run and not grow weary;
   They will walk and not be faint. (Isaiah 40:31)

Part Two: People Somewhat Prepared to Die

Much Better Now

Dave was a friend of fifty years who developed a rare disease. He was admired by many and known by few. His spirit lives on to tell the very human story of hope in the midst of tragedy.

DAVE, MY FRIEND -- DO YOU WANT TO TELL THE STORY OF YOUR DYING?
It was an awful time for me. You had known me for many years, but you did not see the ending of that story. We had so many stories together, but the end of my story was a lonely scene. I had become more and more disappointed with people. This story may be hard for you to write.

THE MAIN THING IS WHAT YOU NEED TO SHARE.
What I need to share may not be interesting reading for everyone. I had pretty much been able to do what I wanted to in life. I was smart enough to get my way. I never had any major defeats in my life. Like the song said, I did it my way. Now, from here, I see that was a narrow way to live. I want to tell people to find a way to not be self-centered.

THE LAST TIME I SAW YOU, I ASKED IF ALL THIS SUFFERING HAD ANY PURPOSE. YOU SAID --"YOUR GRANDSONS." YOU JUST STARED AT ME AFTER YOU SAID THAT. WHAT WAS THAT?
Even though I didn't talk much at the end, I thought more deeply. I knew they were really important to me. I just stared at you because I wanted to say more but couldn't get the words out. I am glad that you asked. I am glad that you and the first boy got along so well. You could joke with him in a way that I couldn't. I was just shutting down mentally.

WAS THE END FOR YOU FOGGY?
Yes. I fell because I couldn't think it all out anymore. I wanted what I wanted and fell down the steps. I was done anyway. Now from this side, I can see it more clearly. I did not have to be foggy; that was my choice really. It's odd the tricks our minds play. It's OK; I was done.

HOW IS IT FOR YOU NOW?
It is brighter. We grew up in an overcast place. It seemed like it was mostly cloudy. It's not like that for me now. I've moved from a foggy place to a bright place.

CAN I BE OF HELP?
Hey, talk to me. We talked for fifty years and then now we don't. I liked that you raked the leaves and visited – but talk to me. I am there too. I know when you are there or the kids are visiting.
   I can be there then. Talk to me; tell me something funny!

PROBABLY MOST OF THE LAUGHS WERE IN OHIO. MY HUMOR WOULD GET US LAUGHING ABOUT MEGAN.
There you go. There is much more humor here -- less serious and more laughs. We don't judge or get serious here. We just live and watch the wheels go around. There is so much to learn here. We were students at the same school; now I am in a new school.

WHAT IS YOUR NEW SCHOOL LIKE?
It is filled with teachers and students who are much more advanced than what we learned back then. I am studying subjects I never knew about before. You might call it astrophysics. I call it the way the universe works. Humans see so little but here there are lessons within lessons for everything.

Part Two: People Somewhat Prepared to Die

What we would talk about would not even qualify as a subject for discussion here.

HOW ARE YOU?
I am much better. Everything has its inherent action and reaction. My healing went better here through the use of light healing. Light is the golden commodity here. There is no sun but much light. Light healed me and heals others.

I SENSE THAT YOU WANT TO OPEN UP A NEW SUBJECT. IS THAT RIGHT?
Yes. The new subject is the new way. Let go of the past and live every day fresh and new. You and other humans live with too much baggage. It's as though you look in your bag of stuff before you act. In your world, the sun comes up every day. Live as though your star is bringing you new life each day. Let go of the old stuff and move forward. That is one thing that dying does for you. It gives you a new view of life. My view now is so different than when I was human. I only saw partially then. Here it is like we live in full light. If you want to see the whole subject, you have to have full lighting.

DO YOU HAVE ANY ADVICE?
Well there is an open invitation for me to be right. Live in the moment. You like Beatle music. Half of them are over here. Which is to say, focus on the music not on the personalities. The music will open up to you every day if you hear with fresh ears. The music is fluid and lively. Focus on the daily sound and not on the human history of the sound. Do that with all of life. That is how we live here. Love often. Give my best and my love to all there. Love really is all you need.

THANKS FOR NOW.

CONTEMPLATION (Dave)
Dave experienced a lonely ending to a diminished life. Read the list below of seven criteria for emotional maturity. Which ones come easy to you? Which ones present a challenge?

The Criteria of Emotional Maturity

1. **The ability to deal constructively with reality.**
2. **The capacity to adapt to change.**
3. **A relative freedom from symptoms that are produced by tensions and anxieties.**
4. **The capacity to find more satisfaction in giving than receiving.**
5. **The capacity to relate to other people in a consistent manner with mutual satisfaction and helpfulness.**
6. **The capacity to sublimate – to direct one's instinctive hostile energy into creative and constructive outlets.**
7. **The capacity to love.**

William C. Menninger, M.D., 1889-1966, Co-founder of the Menninger Clinic

On the other side Dave has found healing, brightness, new subjects to learn, and much more humor. He advises us to let go of old baggage and treat each day as fresh and new. How much old baggage do you have in your life? Make a list and decide what will need to happen for you to let go of each item.

_____
_____
_____
_____

Part Two: People Somewhat Prepared to Die

As you go down the list do you become aware of what you have learned from each one?

One definition of insanity is continuously hoping for a better past. A better past is not going to happen. You have today. Find five things each day that you are grateful for.

_____
_____
_____
_____
_____

If you have love in your life, celebrate it! If you have work that uses your gifts and challenges you, celebrate it! If you have a personal relationship with God, pray with thankfulness!

Dave talks about music that will open up to you if you hear with fresh ears. What music speaks to you and lightens your mood –one example is the hit song "Because I'm Happy" by Pherrell Williams. Generally speaking, most people on earth are as happy as they decide to be. Does that include you?

Part Two: People Somewhat Prepared to Die

Gone Too Soon

Carol was a cancer patient at a large hospital. We met as a patient-chaplain duo would meet in the aftermath of major surgery. She was beloved by her children, her students, and her community. Carol left this world too soon.

I INVITE THE SPIRIT OF CAROL HERE THIS MORNING. WHAT DO YOU WANT TO SHARE ABOUT DYING?
What I know about dying came from my dying. You saw me in the final stages of my cancer suffering. It was so good of you to visit. Though my life had been focused on fun, the end – the dying -- was no fun. I was unprepared for the process of death and thus was full of dread and fear. You provided some hope, but no one else could provide much that was of help at the end. It was pretty awful.

DO YOU HAVE ANY ADVICE FOR US WHO ARE LEFT BEHIND?
My family and you need to carry on. There is so little light on this subject while human. In spirit it is clearer. We have to live and die some way. The more a person knows, the better it goes. That is a rhyme; you can tell that I was fun loving even in the hospital. I still am fun loving. It is just different here. A person gets to be more like what they are here. If only the transition to here was better for people.

HOW COULD THAT BE, CAROL?
You could have a class with a workbook. You could call it pre-grieving. Grieving your death ahead of time would be realistic. It is a loss to lose your life. Work with that ahead of the event. It may be unattractive to most people, but some people would want to get the attention on the lives they had led when it was looking like their life would end. It

could be called: "This was your life." It could be a celebration and a show. Remember when we ......

CAROL, YOU SOUND LIVELY ABOUT THIS. TRUE?
Yes. I was mostly a happy person. I lived and loved the California way of life. I had a husband and children and many friends and family members. Just because cancer got me does not mean that it is all gloom and doom. I am even more who I am now in spirit. I am me and I move amongst humans who think they are alive while we are dead. We really are more alive than most humans. We see more clearly. We live more fully. We are just more alive than you.

GOOD. I AM HAPPY FOR YOU. ONE PHRASE JUMPS OUT AT ME: WHAT DO YOU MEAN THAT CANCER "GOT YOU"?
I have learned that cancer cells are all around. They "get" some people. Some people "get" a cold or flu; others do not. There is the mystery to be worked with. I "got" cancer. Your parents "got" cancer. Why? -- Because that is in the plan for some people. It may sound odd, but cancer is not the problem. What a person does with it is the important part. Some people say they "beat cancer." That is not the whole story. Sometimes a person has to beat cancer. Sometimes those cells have to be befriended. There are many points along the line of how cancer is to be treated. There was a better way for me. Medicine will become much more individual as cancer cells are better understood in their part in the lives of humans. Let's communicate again.

THANK YOU.

Part Two: People Somewhat Prepared to Die

FOR THE SECOND TIME I INVITE IN THE SPIRIT OF CAROL. WHAT DO YOU WANT TO SHARE?
I want to share much. Naturally, I miss my family and friends. I am around them often. You can imagine the state of a mother who has to leave her children behind in the human state. I am more myself here but still miss the human world and all it provides. You may yearn for the spirit life. I would like you to contact my family to let them know that I am fine. But the most important thing is that you write. I want to express to those in the human world.

WHAT DO YOU WANT TO EXPRESS?
As you read, I was a teacher. I was born to teach. My dying was needlessly harsh. Please let other people know that there are options and alternatives for cancer. You have experience with people who do not have a healthy response to cancer like me. Encourage people to seek other ways of reacting to cancer.

WHAT WOULD HAVE BEEN THE BEST WAY FOR YOU?
Thank you for asking. I have studied much and have an advanced level of learning now about cancer. My treatment should have been cooling in nature. You could tell that I was an active person who had many human contacts. My cells were over-heated. My cells could have been cooled down. Hot treatments like radiation are not effective for cells that need to be cooled down. Some cells need that. I did not need harsh chemicals.

HAVE YOU FOUND WHAT YOU DID NEED?
Yes. I studied my case extensively. My type of run-away cancer cells could have been treated with cooling chemicals.

The chemistry for the individual is all important. You are familiar with almond groves. They have a cooling effect on the cells. You have a strong attraction to almonds. Your family has cancer cells. Your family members occasionally run too hot and cells over-heat. You and others innately know what these cells need. Empower patients to know what is best for them.

WOW! THANKS CAROL. THAT IS WHAT I INNATELY LIKE TO DO. CAN YOU HELP?
Sure; I would love to help. Invite me to make rounds with you at the hospital. Pray first and invite me to go on rounds with you. Invite me by name and pray for me and others to go with you. Try it and write about the result. You met me coming out of surgery, but do this especially on the oncology floor. I would love to go along and minister to others who are struggling with cancer cells. Use my lively energy to pierce the cloud that hangs over that unit. Just let go and bring energy into that area that suffers so much from dark thoughts and feelings. Just do it.

THANKS CAROL!

Part Two: People Somewhat Prepared to Die

CONTEMPLATION (Carol)

Because she was unprepared for the final process of dying, Carol was "filled with dread and fear". She wishes this to be different for others. One suggestion she offers is to grieve our losses ahead of time. And there is a lot to grieve as we anticipate our passing. We need to start early during the aging process when the losses begin. Many of us lose all or some of our hearing, our vision, our strength and mental sharpness, memories, friends, and family members. We may lose our independence when we can no longer carry out the activities of daily living (dressing, toileting, bathing, feeding, and walking). It's no wonder that depression is high among the elderly. We need to grieve these losses and we need to grieve to someone who will listen and understand. We want to be heard and we want to retain as much control over our lives as possible. Some will be able to afford assisted living care where there is help with medications and daily living but where there is also privacy and some control over living. What would have to happen for you to be able to get the help you need as you age?

_____
_____
_____
_____

Do you have long term care insurance? Do you have an advance directive or living will that tells your family and doctor what level of treatment you want at the end of your life? Does your physician take time to answer your questions about your health, aging and support system? Ask your doctor what quality of life would be possible if you decide to undergo treatments such as chemotherapy?

How do you want to spend your final days? Use your imagination and picture the best case scenario for your dying. Think about who would be there, what special possessions you would want with you, when your dying might start, where you would want to spend your last day, and how you would choose to die if it was up to you.

_____
_____
_____
_____

Remembering the important events that have happened in our lives is just as useful as grieving our losses. Make a list of the major events in your life; share memories and photo albums with others.

_____
_____
_____
_____

Remember you have learned much over the years and you have the kind of wisdom that only experienced living brings. Also remember as you age and confront losses and disease that you are more than your body and your emotions. Each day do something that comforts you: meditate; pray; have a massage; listen to soothing music; paint a picture; watch a funny movie; read a book. Little by little you will come to realize that while aging can be difficult, you can retain a sense of humor and appreciate those things you can still do and be.

"You don't stop laughing when you grow old; you grow old when you stop laughing."

— George Bernard Shaw

Beloved Clown

The most computer browser searches for 2014 were for Robin Williams. So many of us admired and loved this comic and tragic actor. He lives on in our hearts and memories. Who could have known the pain behind the humor?

I INVITE ROBIN WILLIAMS INTO THIS PLACE TO TALK ABOUT HIS DYING. WHAT DO YOU WANT TO SHARE?
Mine is a spiritual story at the end of a very human life. There were spiritual forces that were too much for me to handle at the end of that fantastic life. I moved from an introverted childhood to an adult life that was too much for me. You can relate to this because we grew up in the same area with similar private lives. Then we went to California for larger lives with more complex human experiments and larger spiritual forces. You had your spiritual practice to ground you. I did not.

The end for me was overwhelming and awful. I just could not handle all my demons with the resources at my disposal. They got the better of me through depression and using. I am going through my life review. I will probably have to go back again.

CAN YOU SAY MORE?
Of course; I could always say more. I followed the advice of my movie character to "seize the day". But carpe diem is only good for the movies. I can see now how each person has to let life come to them. You would say, 'let the game come to you'. I did the opposite. I went looking for ways to have life go my way rather than living life on life's terms. We both learned that phrase. I could not put it into practice. This was the central cause of my "untimely death". Isn't that just the

best phrase? When you take your life into your own hands of course it is untimely. It wasn't my time yet. I will be working that out with the help of others. I really appreciate all the support from around the world. Thanks for your prayers.

DOES BEING A BIG MOVIE STAR HELP IN THE SPIRITUAL LIFE?
It does to the extent that you get love and grace from the hearts of people; but no, not really.

In my case being a movie star led me away from being real. The universe just is as it is. If I tried to make it better, that would just mess up the picture. In my case we will have to do another take I am afraid.

DO YOU HAVE ANY ADVICE?
Sure. Be yourself. I got away from that over time. You would be surprised at what my life plan was about. You could guess that I was meant to be a performer and a public speaker; just not that Hollywood kind. I got lost along the way. I am still who I am, but I have baggage to go with that. Humans don't get lost because of ninety degree turns usually. It is more a series of two degree turns that leads to being lost in the weeds. There is a hint.

I USED YOUR "ROBIN WILLIAMS LIVE" TAPE FOR THOUSANDS OF HOURS.
That's ironic, yeah. I knew drugs backwards and forwards, but never really left them alone. I thought I could use them a little; while they were really using me. I never would have ended my life clean and sober. Live and learn! Next time I may not be able to use them as a way to cope. Any one for life as an aborigine in the outback?

YOU STILL HAVE YOUR SENSE OF HUMOR.

"Of course; it is still me, and it is very much "

— Robin Williams Live".

Part Two: People Somewhat Prepared to Die

CONTEMPLATION (Robin Williams)
Trying to control life instead of "living life on life's terms" kept Robin Williams "from being real". What does he mean by this? Being real means honoring our personality, our beliefs, our values, our true feelings, our perspectives on the world around us, and our honesty in interactions with others. When we go against these important things that contribute to our individuality, we behave the way we think others want (or wanted) us to behave. As Williams says, doing this repeatedly leads us away from being real.

Many of us were raised with rules and requirements to be a certain way. The love we received was conditional and did not meet our needs. We weren't listened to, accepted, and loved as a unique being. Consider those things that make you, you; those things that make you feel authentic. Write down some examples. What helps you to be real? What keeps you from being yourself?

_____
_____
_____
_____
_____
_____

Lost "in the weeds" and believing himself in control of his drug addiction, Williams found he could not control all his "demons". Because he was such a public person we know about some of these – the alcohol and drugs, his depression, his Parkinson diagnosis. But no one can totally know another's internal demons.

By definition when we are addicted, we cannot control that addiction by ourselves, without help. Asking for help is a healthy way to manage addictive diseases, as the many twelve step programs have shown. But asking for help is very difficult for many people. Contrary to what we sometimes tell ourselves, asking for help does not mean we are weak; it means we can do together with others those things (like recovery) that we cannot do alone. When have you asked for help in your life? Did you ask God too?

_____
_____
_____
_____
_____
_____
_____

> **"THE FOUR-FOLD WAY: SHOW UP FOR LIFE; PAY ATTENTION; SPEAK YOUR TRUTH; DON'T GET ATTACHED TO THE RESULTS."**
>
> — ANGELES ARRIEN, 1940-2014

The Good Wife

Jacqueline Bouvier Kennedy was considered by many to be the model First Lady. And yet, what a surprise it is to read about the true spiritual nature of this private person. She presents no interest in returning to the tumultuous human life that she has left behind.

I INVITE HERE NOW, THE SPIRIT OF JACQUELINE KENNEDY. WHAT WOULD YOU LIKE TO SHARE?
This work that you do is for the well-being of many. Make it available to many and some will accept it and prosper from it. The important part for you is to persevere in this writing process. Continue on.

I APPRECIATE THE ENCOURAGEMENT. MANY OF US WOULD WANT TO KNOW ABOUT YOU. WHAT DO YOU WANT TO SHARE?
I appreciate your concern and sensitivity in your question. I was a private person who was thrust into world-wide notoriety. It was part of my life plan, but not to my liking as a human. My role as support to the Kennedy family soon blossomed into greater responsibilities. To me it seemed like one challenge met turned into another challenge to be addressed and fulfilled.

MANY ADMIRE YOUR PEACEFUL MANNER
That was a studied approach to meeting one's responsibilities in life. My early life was training for the demands of adult life. I was fully prepared for the demands that the public life presented, but I never actually enjoyed it. It was a life of meeting demands and surviving for another day. You may not know this, but I did not divulge my whole life in a book. Even though I spent my last years as an editor, I

never presented all my inner life to the world. That was not my way.

ARE THERE ANY DETAILS THAT YOU DO WANT TO SHARE?
Yes, I am less protected now. That human life is complete. I do appreciate your prayers during my dying. The Kennedy family was always protective of me and solicitous for my well-being. Your prayers and the prayers of others helped my transition into spirit. My life here is more to my liking. I write and enjoy the life of peace that the human life never afforded me.

DO YOU HAVE CONTACT WITH THE KENNEDY'S THERE?
That would always be the popular question. They are more a clannish group that works together. The four brothers, the parents, the ancestors – they all group together here in spirit too. I was not a Kennedy and am not part of that group now. In spirit we are all connected, but not in the way that humans think. I enjoy gardening and writing.

FASCINATING. DO YOU HAVE ANY LAST SHARING?
I appreciate that you wanted to include a famous American woman, but I do not savor this. I may not respond again. I am on to my authentic spiritual life and may not want to go back to that time of turmoil for me and so many. You will understand that not everyone has a taste for the cutting edge. I would refer you to other human women who had, and have, a taste for that sort of thing.

THANK YOU.

CONTEMPLATION (Jacqueline Kennedy Onassis)
Her spirit speaks to us from the other side where she now lives a quiet, peaceful and "authentic" life. She writes and gardens and shuns any intrusion into her new life. She has certainly earned this peace, having survived much trauma while she lived on earth. Prior to her husband's assassination, she had two children who died, a daughter stillborn and a son who lived only two days.

Jackie Kennedy was one of our most popular first ladies, noted for her style, elegance, grace, and intellect. She is known best for her restoration of the White House. She is quoted as saying: "I feel so strongly that the White House should have as fine a collection of American pictures as possible. It's so important... the setting in which the presidency is presented to the world, to foreign visitors. The American people should be proud of it. We have such a great civilization. So many foreigners don't realize it. I think this house should be the place we see them (the pictures) best." When the restoration was complete, she led a televised tour through the mansion and the film of the tour was distributed to 106 countries around the world.

Continuing her dedication to preserving the Kennedy presidency for history, Jackie also worked on the Kennedy Library in Boston, Massachusetts. It remains a lasting legacy of the accomplishments achieved during that time.

What does a lasting legacy mean to you? Are there family heirlooms you want to pass down to others?

_____
_____
_____
_____
_____
_____

Part Two: People Somewhat Prepared to Die

In addition to possessions, you will leave a legacy of the choices you have made during your lifetime and the decisions you made that are uniquely yours. Review your major life events and make a timeline of these and of how you feel about them. Some people draw their timelines; others clip pictures from magazines to group together to represent the major milestones of their life; others make a scrapbook. Take your time; don't try to complete your timeline in one sitting.

Start with your childhood. Who and what stands out as contributing to your growth?

_____
_____
_____
_____

Continue on into young adulthood; what challenges did you meet? What did you find to be overwhelming or particularly satisfying during these years?

_____
_____
_____
_____

Continue into adulthood and note the challenges and milestones during these years. As you age, do you see personal changes happening along the way? Do you feel you are still the person you were in the past or have you developed into someone who is different in certain ways?

_____
_____
_____
_____

Include your plans, hopes, and ideas for the future in the timeline.
_____
_____
_____
_____

When you feel your timeline is complete, share it with at least one other person.
　　Write down what the process has been like for you.
_____
_____
_____
_____

Both Human and Spiritual

Thomas Merton was the most popular Christian writer of the twentieth century. And yet, even he found that balancing the body, mind, and spirit was challenging. He encourages us to try to balance all three of our natures while still human.

I INVITE THE SPIRIT OF THOMAS MERTON TODAY. HOW WAS YOUR DYING?
It was such a silly death. I was distracted in my thinking and touched the electric fan. I knew better, but I was really not paying attention. And in a greater way, I was ready to go on. You mention the death of Raymond Brown as being sudden because he was called to something greater. It was similar for me. The human realm can only hold so much. So, I was called on to another level of living. The electric shock was quick and final. I saw my body fall away and I was still present. It was only a moment in time and I was on to greater living.

WHAT IS YOUR LIFE LIKE NOW?
It is similar to a pasture land where I lived. I write and pray much as before. Because the light is stronger here, the essence of my writing is richer and clearer. I enjoy writing more in spirit.

WHAT ARE YOU WRITING?
You would probably not understand the subtle nature of this writing. Human life is denser than spirit life. There you struggle for every part of life. Here, life is an ever-present gift with great abundance. My human writing focused on truth and justice. The same applies here, but the content here is finer and more helpful to the life of the individual person. For example, you know that you enjoy a story. In

books or movies, you appreciate a story well told. Here in spirit, the stories are much richer and fuller. For example, "The Seven Story Mountain"(1948 autobiography) would be a better story here. The facts of the story would be better, the words would be richer, and the depth of the story more complete.

HOW ABOUT YOU AND LOVE -- YOU AND THE NURSE?
Wow! Everyone wants to know about that part of my life story. It was a gift to us, but that world could not hold the experience. There were too many facts in the way of just enjoying the experience of love. I appreciated the gift of love in life, but it disturbed too many others. It was part of my passing. It was so hard to reconcile love with truth in that strict world. God is always bringing new gifts into life to bring us closer to life. That was a gift that we did not know how to use well. You understand the concept. It has happened to you too. Live and learn in light and love.

DO YOU HAVE ANY OTHER ADVICE THAT YOU WANT TO SHARE?
There is so much that I want to share. Let's start small and see where we go from humble beginnings. You have just come back from talking to a fellow seeker in spiritual living. That process is a gift to you and her. Not many humans get this urge to go into the spiritual part of life while still a human person. Encourage body, mind, and spirit. Just the willingness to address the subject of spirit will help others to see the spirit within them. And, in the end, that is the central movement of humans in their lives —to move from body to mind to spirit. In some ways it is simpler and easier here. We are pure spirits. Humans must balance the three natures in one person. Humans have a more complex

life because of these three natures in one person. Humans have physical needs while experiencing mental wants and spiritual yearnings. That will do for a start. Peace.

Part Two: People Somewhat Prepared to Die

CONTEMPLATION (Thomas Merton)
Thomas Merton was a Trappist monk, writer, and civil rights advocate. He tells us to focus on truth and justice. Spend some time reading newspapers or magazines and listening to the news. What examples do you find of truth in the world and in your everyday life?

_____
_____
_____
_____
_____

What examples do you find of justice in the world and in your own life?

_____
_____
_____
_____
_____

Merton also tells us to prepare for eternity by moving from body (our senses) to mind (our rational thinking) to spirit (our belief, trust, and love of a higher power). Write a positive affirmation for your body, mind, and spirit. For example:

- <u>Body</u> = I feel strength in my body and trust each part of my body to perform the work it needs to do.
- <u>Mind</u> = My mind is able to think through and resolve the problems I encounter in life.
- <u>Spirit</u> = My spirit worships a power greater than myself with love and thankfulness.

Write each affirmation on a sheet of paper and tape each in a place where you will see them every day.

At the end of each day, think of how you spent your time and energy using your body, your mind, and your spirit. Over time can you see yourself spending more and more time nurturing your spirit through prayer and meditation and contemplation? Know that when you talk to the God of your understanding throughout your day you are preparing to live in God's kingdom in your next life.

> ***"Love the Lord your God with all your heart and with all your soul and with all your strength and with all your mind."***
>
> — Luke 10:27

More Life Next

Raymond Brown was a noted author who was responsible for both "Death of the Messiah" and "Birth of the Messiah." His writing style was encyclopedic and included long sections on the intentional death of the Messiah, Ya Shua of Judea. We use the words Jesus Christ to name the Messiah who lived and died two thousand years ago in the Middle East. Though Dr. Brown's writing was well researched, his death came with the suddenness that can frighten us all.

I INVITE IN THE SPIRIT OF THE AUTHOR RAYMOND BROWN. CAN YOU SHARE THE STORY OF YOUR DYING?
I was getting to the end of my life and my writing. I sensed and knew that my life force was ebbing. It was just a matter of time before I was going to die. I was mostly at peace and reconciled to the idea of dying, but the actual day of dying was very distressful. I was not ready to let go personally.

DO YOU HAVE ANY ADVICE FOR PEOPLE STILL IN THEIR BODY?
Yes, Prepare for the process of leaving the body joyfully and easily. It is not like any other experience. Prepare by focusing on the spirit through meditation and prayer.

WHAT IS YOUR AFTERLIFE LIKE?
There could be a better word than afterlife. It is the continuation of life in another form. It could be considered as life 2.0. It is life, and there is more added in the new body that does not have the hindrance of the physical body. I am still Raymond, but there is so much more of me now that I am in spirit. I spend my days writing and researching like before, but at a better level. I have bigger libraries to work

with, and thus I have better things to write. <u>Death of the Messiah</u> was just a beginning actually. His death was so much grander than that book portrays. It was a death that was planned out ahead of time, and had to be lived out for the greater glory of God. It is like the man born blind story. A seeming tragedy was actually for the glory of God; it was the way that God wanted it to be.

CAN WE HUMANS KNOW THE PURPOSE OF OUR LIVES?
Yes. Just as Jesus had a dying script prepared, so does each human. Through contemplation the records can be read. That sort of death has meaning and purpose and tends to the greater glory of God. Your death can be that way. It can be a public death that has meaning for others. You can, as Jesus did, tell people ahead of time that you will die at a certain time in a certain place. That would be a sign to others. You can do that. You are already starting that process. You tell people that you are checking out at age 88. That is because you have seen the records and know that is your life span. It is long and full but not too long. You have much work to do to get to that point. It will be twenty years from now.

WOW! THE RECORDS ARE THAT PRECISE?
Yes. Humans don't know this, but human lives are very proscribed for the greater honor and glory of God. A human agrees to this life before life begins and then either follows through on God's plan for glory or not. Looking at it that way, we can either keep our promise to God or not. It's that simple. We can be wise enough to travel the path in God's way, or go off on our own way. It really is simple. The way of living is open to every human. Either we adhere to the script set out for us or we do not. Either we are true to the

life, or we are not. Either we journey through our life staying on the path set out for us or we wander off our path.

THANK YOU DR. BROWN.

CONTEMPLATION (Raymond Brown)

What would you feel if you knew without a doubt that your dying moment would be joyful and peaceful. Take time and try to picture that. Consider that no matter how your body has suffered up to that time the final moment will require no struggle at all; you will simply feel relaxed and joyful and look forward to slipping into a new spiritual body. Even better, you will still be you in the next world and you will be able to continue those things that are meaningful to you.

Neurologist and psychiatrist Viktor Frankl survived the concentration camps of the Holocaust and came to believe that humans' primary motivation is to search for meaning in life. Meaning, he said, can be found in three ways: l) by creating something or doing a deed; 2) by experiencing something or encountering someone; and 3) by the attitude we take toward unavoidable suffering. Read those three ways again. Write examples of what has made your life meaningful so far.

_____
_____
_____
_____
_____

Do your examples help you recognize a plan for your life? Are you "wise enough to travel your path in God's way"? Consider saying this simple prayer every day: *God help me to know your will for my life and give me the power to carry that out.*

Do you believe your lifespan has been predetermined and through prayer and meditation you can come to know when you will die? How long do you want to live? Where do you go to ponder questions like these?

_____
_____
_____
_____

In The Woods

— Kay Talbot

**In the woods I share my burdens
with the birds above and the creek below.
I lift up my eyes to the giant redwoods,
standing tall and strong.
In the woods I empty my worries
and remind myself that no matter what
the water rolls over the rocks,
prepared for whatever comes next.
In the woods I see the chipmunks
darting around in search of food.
I smell the deep green grasses
and breathe in God's healing grace.**

Part Three: People Prepared to Die

In this section we encounter people who invested time and attention into the process of leaving this human life. They prepared for death with a purpose that made sense to them. Their stories are inspiring accounts of how we slip into spirit with intent and awareness.

The Good Nurse

My aunt M was the most beloved member of my family when I was growing up. She was always wise and kind and present. She touched so many patients as a nurse for 40 years, and she still helps me as I walk the halls of the big hospitals.

I INVITE THE SPIRIT OF MY AUNT M.: DO YOU WANT TO SHARE THE STORY OF YOUR DYING?
I really was prepared for my last days on earth. They went quickly and I moved easily to the other side of life. I had many family and friends to help me pass over. I was inspired by spiritual writings all my life and was faithful to the church. I really was not too thrown off, but I was surprised by the beauty here.

CAN YOU TELL ABOUT THE SURPRISE OF LIVING ON THE OTHER SIDE?
Humans see so little because of the body. When the body is no longer a hindrance, we see with the spiritual eyes. It really is awesomely beautiful. Everything in spirit has an

essence that is so much more pure and whole than any worldly ways.

ARE YOU GROUNDED IN SPIRIT?
Yes, this is who I really am here. You remember some of my human ways. I no longer am hindered by the ways of the body. Here, we are who we are.

I AM RESISTING ASKING YOU ABOUT THINGS THAT I REMEMBER. YOU WERE SO IMPORTANT TO ME GROWING UP. I REMEMBER GOING TO SLEEP THINKING YOU WERE THE ONLY ONE WHO UNDERSTOOD LIFE. I FEEL LIKE MY GRATITUDE AND LOVE FOR YOU MAY GET IN THE WAY OF MY BEING A SCRIBE.
Quite the opposite: Your love helps the connection. I could see early that you had a spiritual way. That is why you would feel relieved when I would visit. You could sense that spiritual connection. I wish I could have taught you more. But I was trying to survive myself in that cynical and strict time. It was not possible to speak out then. The life of a spiritual woman has not always been easy. I prayed for you, but couldn't talk openly. I told your mother some things, but she also was under the strict influence.

I AM SORRY THAT IT WAS HARSH FOR YOU AND OTHERS.
That is why this way of life is such a relief for me and many. Here we not only get to be who we are, but we live in spirit. If we are interested in healing, we get to live that way. If we are interested in teaching, we get to live that way.

I AM HAPPY FOR YOU IN SPIRIT. I AM GRATEFUL THAT IT IS BETTER IN SPIRIT.
Gratitude is the currency in both realms. Being grateful for what is helps the human condition and the spiritual life. All comes from one source, and that source loves to be thanked and appreciated. I have learned to call that source, God. So I thank God for what is.

I AM THINKING SO MUCH ABOUT OUR FAMILY. I TRUST THAT YOU HAVE A CLEARER PICTURE ABOUT ALL THIS NOW.
Yes. You came out of a mixed family. Family to you is a complex subject. There were many varied influences in your early life. It was confusing for you. I knew your maternal side. There was much love and connection there. Your maternal side is still connected in the spirit world. Your grandparents and most of the family chose to stay together on this side. Your prayers for your ancestors are much appreciated. They are like gifts to them. It really is like a delivery of gifts coming up to us every day as you would mark time. Usually it is spirit who helps humans. We give loving intentions for those still struggling on earth in your hard world. When you give to us, it is a pleasant surprise.

IT BRINGS ME TO TEARS THAT I CAN HELP YOU AFTER YOU WERE SO MUCH HELP TO ME AS A CHILD.
From our point of view, you are all children. You mostly don't see or understand life. You are so hindered by the body. Though you still are childlike in your understanding,

you have meditation that allows you to see a bit. You can see that you are happier when you get away from body living and get into spirit living. I, and we, encourage you to live that way.

THANK YOU. ANY OTHER MESSAGES FOR US KIDS?
You always did have a cheeky sense of humor. You know most humans didn't understand it, but the family does. You need to make the choices that are best for your spiritual life now. You are not that far from spirit, so you would be best off focusing on spiritual living now. Your meditation is helpful. Your prayer is helpful. Your caring for people is both a blessing and a curse. Let God do the caring and you do the asking. Your helping is effective when you ask God to do it rather than think that you are doing it. Your hospital residency was great because you let go and let God. Did you notice how well you got along with the nurses – especially the charge nurses? Who in your family was a nurse? Who walked those halls with you?

ONCE AGAIN I AM BROUGHT TO TEARS. THE ANSWER WOULD BE YOU. THANKS!

Part Three: People Prepared to Die

CONTEMPLATION (Aunt M.)
What joy it can bring to hear from a loved one who has passed on to the other side. Aunt M. says that there we see with spiritual eyes and are surprised by a beauty we cannot see while in our bodies. She says she had an easy passing. But she did not have an easy life on Earth. She talks of living in a cynical, overly strict time. Families often had rules such as: Don't talk; don't feel; don't trust. Be perfect. Make the right impression. You are what you do. You're only lovable if you're good. When this happens, we are left with a lot of emotional damage. Did this happen to you? Write down any rules that your family had or has. Were they helpful or hurtful for you?

_____
_____
_____
_____

Emotional damage is something we all need to heal inside ourselves. We cannot change others but in order to find peace we can forgive others who have hurt us. Forgiving does not mean condoning insensitive or abusive behavior, or trusting those who are not trustworthy. Forgiving is something you do for yourself to find serenity. It dissolves anger like an antacid. It is a way of looking at others as being unable to love and cherish you in the ways you needed. You forgive the person, not the act. Those who ask and receive forgiveness from others, from God, and from themselves become able to live their remaining days with greater freedom than ever before. Forgiveness sets your spirit free. Compose a prayer for the forgiveness you need to give and receive.

_____
_____
_____
_____

How much easier life is for those who believe they are surrounded by guardian spirits that are like Aunt M. We can send prayers of remembrance as gifts to our spirit guides. Do you think there is, or could be, someone from the spirit world who walks this life with you? Write a special memory you have about that person and what he or she means to you. Do you have a photo you'd like to include?

_____
_____
_____
_____

In the rising of the sun and in its going down, we remember them. In the blowing of the wind and in the chill of winter, we remember them. In the opening of the buds and in the rebirth of spring, we remember them. In the blueness of the sky and in the warmth of summer, we remember them. In the rustling of leaves and in the beauty of autumn, we remember them. In the beginning of the year and when it ends, we remember them. When we are lost and sick at heart we remember them. When we have joys we yearn to share we remember them. So long as we live they too shall live, for they are now a part of us as we remember them.

— From the Gates of Prayer: Reformed Judaism Prayer Book

Light for Living

If every family has a saint, my Grandma was ours. Faithful, long-suffering, joyful – those were the qualities of my Grandma. She is still a light in the darkness for me in this human drama.

I INVITE GRANDMA ELLEN, MY FATHER'S MOTHER, IN THIS MORNING. GRANDMA, CAN YOU TELL US ABOUT YOUR DYING?

It was so simple that I hardly knew that it happened. At ninety-four I did not have a strong connection with my body. I slipped into the other side and was aware that the room looked different and that I could see spirits and people at the same time. That was my first surprise. There was so much more in the room. They never had been there before from my point of view.

WHAT WAS THE PHYSICAL SENSATION OF DYING LIKE FOR YOU?

It was like slipping out of the body. I do not have a way to say it humanly. At one instant I was how I always felt and the next I was looking down at my body. The sensation was a feeling of freedom. That body had worn out and I slipped out of it into a way that was lighter. I felt less heavy, and thus lighter, and all was brighter; that kind of light when the sun comes into a room.

CAN YOU DESCRIBE THOSE WHO WERE IN THE ROOM WITH YOU WHEN YOU BECAME FREE?

There were different types of spirits. Some would be called angels and some would be called people who I knew before who were now in spirit. It was not all that startling for me because I had seen them in dreams and visions toward the end. I had been detaching for a while because I was so frail and in bed. Dying was simple and natural for me.

IS THERE ANY ADVICE FOR THOSE WHO ARE STILL IN THE BODY?
You remember me as a simple older woman who you didn't have much in common with. As a boy you could not see who I was beyond the difference in our human ways. Actually, we are similar. I appreciate that you pray to me daily now. We have more in common now than when we were related by family. I would advise people to look deeper at who they are living with. People are the most advanced forms in life, yet humans just notice the surface. I would advise all to see the spirit in each other. Each soul is unique. Get to know that soul better than the body because the body just acts as the container for spirit.

HOW CAN HUMANS DO THAT?
I gave you the line; "What do you most want me to know about you?" You have said it many times. Has it always worked to get people to open up? Has it taken the talk deeper than the surface life? Do real questions bring connection better than just statements?

YES, I SEE YOUR POINT. WE ALL WANT TO TELL OUR STORY.
Most want to tell their story. Some want to keep secrets to keep control. Encourage people to tell their secrets. At the hospital you love to hear, "I have never told anyone this before." Why? You can feel how freeing it is for people.

HONESTLY GRANDMA, I NEVER KNEW THAT YOU WERE SO WISE. I AM SORRY THAT I MISSED YOU.

You didn't see because you had things to work out. Some children see clearly, but most don't. We see each other better now. You ask me for light for the journey; you are getting close to the light.

I SAY THAT YOU ARE THE SAINT IN THIS FAMILY. IS THAT TRUE?
Your human words are not precise. Saint is a word with many meanings. I do not believe that I will be born again. My guides have put me on a path that is consistent with the new body that I have. The best way I can say it to you is that I have a glorified body. It will not go down into being incarnated. You may not understand that, but it shows a picture about the state I am in. My focus is on going up to another state next.

DO YOU WANT TO TEACH ME ABOUT THAT?
Of course, but you have more basic lessons to learn first. Keep asking me every day for help and light and things will progress. You have guides and angels also that want to help you. The best for you now is to let go of the human and body power. It is unusual I know. It will become easier as you mature. I am not saying you are a child; but in comparison we still have the same way between us. I am the elder and you are the learner.

THANK YOU. I AM SO GRATEFUL.
There is more to share later.

Part Three: People Prepared to Die

CONTEMPLATION (Grandma Ellen)

When a loved one returns to reassure us all is well and we believe the messages given, we mostly feel relieved and hopeful (*see below). The natural fear of dying falls away and we look toward what the experience will be for us. From the compilation of near death experiences, including those of children, several common experiences have been described: the tunnel; the bright light; the feeling of free floating – looking down at the body. At her death grandma Ellen was surprised to see both people and spiritual beings at her bedside.

Some people feel strongly they have angels and guides helping them during this life. Is this true for you? Dreams and visions may bring us surprising insights prior to death. Keep index cards or this workbook beside your bed so you can quickly write them down. Describe what happened in the dream and how you feel about it.

_____
_____
_____
_____

Ellen urges us not to hold onto our secrets. The common phrase "we are only as sick as our secrets" alludes to how important it is to unburden ourselves of those things that make us feel guilty, angry, embarrassed, or ashamed. Do you have someone in your life you would be able to confide in about things that trouble you? If not, find a counselor, priest, rabbi, or minister who can help with this.

---

*After death communications, called ADCs, occur when someone is contacted spontaneously and directly by a deceased family member or friend without the help of a medium. Research shows that these spiritual experiences offer hope, love, and comfort for thousands of people. Hello from Heaven, 1996, Bill and Judy Guggenheim.

___

___

___

"Look deeper at who you are living with," and "see the spirit in each other," she says. Often we know our likes and dislikes, our skills and capabilities, and our shortcomings. But do we really know the essence of one another's soul? For these we need descriptive words. Some examples: she has a generous heart; he is sympathetic; she/he is loving, considerate, affectionate, gentle, gracious, charitable, kind, welcoming, unselfish, curious, etc. At funerals people talk a lot about the kind of person he or she was and not as much about how successful or powerful the person was. What words would you like people to use to describe you at your funeral? Make a list.

___

___

___

___

___

Dying Doctor

Some doctors have a way of moving the discussion forward. Dr. Elizabeth Kubler-Ross was one of those doctors. She brought into focus the topic of dying in our time.

I INVITE IN THE SPIRIT OF ELIZABETH KUBLER-ROSS. HOW WAS YOUR DYING PROCESS?
It was as frustrating as could be. After all my work and writing, I was having the kind of death I did not want. After working through the ways of the mind, my mind, or technically, my brain did not serve me well. It was a frustrating transition that could have been smoother.

DO YOU WANT TO SHARE YOUR ADVICE?
Meditate and contemplate more. A person can never be too prepared for such a profound experience. The life of the body and mind fall away rapidly at the time of dying. The spirit must be prepared to acknowledge itself in the moment of dying. If the spirit is not prepared, there is reluctance for the human part of a person to let go completely. That was my experience. As much as I knew about the human experience of dying from work in hospitals, the nature of the spirit was not completely known to me. I could have been better prepared for the dying experience from a spiritual point of view.

WHAT WISDOM DO YOU WANT TO SHARE?
I have learned much as I have progressed in spirit. I liked going to schools and hospitals to study when I was in human form. I still do. I go to greater places to learn about the ways of the spiritual realm that I live in now. The basic wisdom to share is that there is less fear and more joy here because we do not worry about death or dying. We simply

live. There, you have to work through dying. Here, we have the knowledge that we go on and on.

LET'S START THERE.
Perhaps I could tell a story to make the point about the difference between human and spirit. What if you never had to worry about getting old, getting sick, money, or what others thought of you? What if you were, who you were? It was that simple. You never worried about the body or the mind, but just lived as you really are. Would living seem better? Would the troublesome parts of living seem less troublesome? Of course; that is what living is like here. We don't worry. We don't fear. Life is as it is. If a human could take that perspective, life would be lived more realistically. Living could be a simpler experience. Each person could have the faith that they will go on and on into the future. The future becomes more of an adventure than a scary journey or trip. Learning to trust in the future is the missing link. Learning to prepare for dying as a spiritual adventure is a truer way of dying than worrying and fretting in ignorance.

WHAT WOULD YOU ADVISE US TO DO?
Prepare. Find a dying story that makes sense to you and put it into action well before dying. It would be like the Make a Wish Foundation for children, but it would be for every human being to put into action for themselves. Going to Heaven? Start the process. Going to be with loved ones? Start the process. Going to Paradise City? Start the process. Encourage people to start their process.

CONTEMPLATION (Elizabeth Kubler-Ross)
As the first to identify five stages that dying people often go through (denial; anger; bargaining; depression; and acceptance), Kubler-Ross became world-renowned. But at her death the many years of study, practice, and writing did not help her to let go of her body and easily move into spirit. She tells us to meditate and contemplate and view dying as a "spiritual adventure."

For those who have never tried to meditate or contemplate, this is no easy task. Meditate, by definition, means to quiet our minds while we reflect and ponder our spirit (see Guided Meditation in Part Four). When we contemplate we are examining, considering, and mulling over what has been said; written; seen; felt; or heard and comparing our findings with our current attitude about life. Has your attitude about life changed over the years? What has seemed to cause any changes you have experienced about life? Do you believe that your destiny is pre-determined?

_____
_____
_____
_____

Would your answers be different if you knew you were not going to die, that you would live forever?
In what ways would your answers change?

_____
_____
_____
_____

Some people make up a list of experiences they want to have or accomplishments they want to complete before dying.

Part Three: People Prepared to Die

The 2007 movie "Bucket List" starring Jack Nicholsen and Morgan Freeman provides good examples. If you haven't seen the film, arrange to rent or buy it. Think about what you would want to include on your own bucket list. (Mine includes finishing this book!)

_____
_____
_____
_____

Another way of acknowledging your spirit is to write down those things that give you vitality and improve your mood. Make a list.

_____
_____
_____
_____

Serenity Prayer

> *God, grant me the serenity to accept the things I cannot change, courage to change the things I can, and the wisdom to know the difference. Living one day at a time; enjoying one moment at a time; accepting hardship as the pathway to peace. Taking, as He did, this sinful world as it is, not as I would have it. Trusting that He will make all things right if I surrender to His will; that I may be reasonably happy in this life, and supremely happy with Him forever in the next. Amen.*
>
> — Reinhold Niebuhr

Part Three: People Prepared to Die

Change of Direction

George Harrison moved through new directions in his large life. He moved from rock star to yogi. And yet in the end he mostly wanted to talk about real love.

I INVITE IN THE SPIRIT OF GEORGE HARRISON. GEORGE, HOW WAS YOUR DYING PROCESS?
It was blessed by many in spirit and humans. I knew I was physically dying over a long period of time. The actual moment was like slipping into another sphere altogether. Immediately everything looked and felt different. I was lighter and freer than ever before.

IS THERE ANYTHING ELSE THAT YOU WANT TO SHARE?
Yes, the idea I had of wanting to become a (Hindu) yogi while I was still a pop star. It was a huge transition for me to move from Beatle to Bodhisattva (an enlightened being). I tried my best but there was so much to undo.

HOW WAS YOUR LIFE REVIEW?
Very long. I had so much to reevaluate from this life that was so varied. I got my wish to move in the spiritual direction and leave all that behind. I will have to start at the bottom and work through the process of becoming truly spiritual. I knew some of the words, but the actual feeling of spirit is entirely different. I feel like I feel, but it is a bit like having amnesia from what I used to feel like.

DO YOU HAVE ANY ADVICE?
Yes. Meditate much. It predisposes the person to feel like a spirit feels. It is a bit dreamy and not like thinking like a computer. Living in spirit is more immediate and less dense.

A thought or feeling is thicker as a human than as a spirit. Meditate.

DO YOU HAVE ANY INSIGHTS FROM THE LIFE YOU LED?
Don't just sing about love, but actually love. It is an action of the heart and not just the voice or the thinking. Real loving takes much commitment to that which is loved. It is easier to love a bunny than to love the universe, but the concept is the same. You feel a oneness with that which you love and love all the time. We (the Beatles) just sang about a little bit of love. But love is like a jewel with many facets.

A person needs to love all the facets of that which is loved. Partial love is just loving some of the facets. The greatest story ever told, or the greatest song ever sung, would be about a complete love.

DO YOU HAVE AN EXAMPLE FROM SPIRIT?
It would be a whole life that was committed to love. It would not be just three minutes long or year- long but life-long. The best object of love is reality. A person could love the reality of the moments of life. Just loving the entirety of experience would be the greatest message. To love oneself, in one's environment in its entirety, in the greater universe would be the greatest experience. What do you love? How are you loved? What fills your experience with love?

Part Three: People Prepared to Die

CONTEMPLATION (George Harrison)
What would it be like to devote oneself to "a whole life committed to love"? It could start with learning to love all facets of God and yourself. Harrison offers these questions: What do you love? How are you loved? What fills your experience with love? Write down your answers.

_____
_____
_____
_____
_____

Do you feel a oneness with that which you love? How would this work when the one who is loved is very different from you and at times is a challenge to love at all? Can you allow that person to be different but as worthy of love as you are? Can you honor your love commitment by holding your tongue and acknowledging the other person's right to their point of view? Think of examples when you were able to do this and write them down.

_____
_____
_____
_____
_____

Harrison also advises us to meditate (see Guided Meditation in Part Four). Is this something you could make a commitment to do as a daily practice? Think of this as the practice of putting your mind to rest by turning off the computer of your brain and floating free without thoughts or ideas. This is a dedication to openness. Someone once said not to worry about keeping an open mind because nothing really important will fall out. When you meditate you are not missing out on this life; you are preparing yourself for your next life.

> *"Meditation is a way for nourishing and blosoming the divinity within you."*
>
> — Dr. Amit Ray, Indian author and spiritual master.

Dying Like A Saint

The story below describes a way of dying that was followed by a religious person. This woman had prepared for death in a way that was religiously informed. She had the death of her Savior to act as a model for her dying. Her dying included a clear intention, a strong spiritual practice, and a proscribed goal for her dying. She had lived a public life where her dying process was public information that could be examined. She had written extensively during her lifetime about her spiritual life and her human experiences.

TERESA OF CALCUTTA IS INVITED TO SHARE HER DYING STORY.
My dying was very small. I was as prepared as a person could be for so momentous a time. I slipped away after going upstairs for a rest. It was as though things were unplugged within me. I could feel myself slipping away. Though I had prayed and had prepared mentally, the moment of dying was like nothing else. I was leaving, and I knew that I would not come back as who I had been.

IS THERE ANY ADVICE YOU WANT TO SHARE ABOUT DYING?
For each person there should be a preparation for so deep an experience. It is like nothing else that a human can even imagine. Naturally, one should have their relationships, especially with God, in order. It is such a tumultuous time that all should be ready for that moment of passing out of the body. Nothing should be left to chance. All should be made ready.

HOW DID YOU MAKE READY?
Communion with our Lord was most important for me. Communion was my daily focus and my main thought.

Part Three: People Prepared to Die

People may be of help, but our Lord was central to my every thought and act. All else seemed trivial. What had been so important during my working life became not interesting. Those plans and thoughts drifted away in comparison to my focus on our Lord. He died also, so I trusted in his dying. His mother died, too, so I trusted in her dying.

IS THERE ANYTHING THAT SURPRISED YOU ABOUT YOUR DYING TIME?
It was the unplugging process. All that I held so dear and all that had seemed so important was losing its connection. All was just drifting away. I was surprised by the dramatic change in how I felt and thought. I would have prepared better for the deep change if I had been aware of the difference that dying makes. I was letting go whether I wanted to or not.

HAVE YOU LEARNED ANYTHING AFTER DEATH?
I have learned the great difference of our human life and our spiritual life. In our human life we are so limited in our view. The view is limited by the body. The body and its senses are so loud that they can overwhelm the spirit. It is easier to be spiritual after the body is no longer attached. I have learned that everything has a deeper essence. In spirit we see the thing itself. In the body we see a surface reflection of the thing. This is true of people or plants. There is a deeper essence.

HOW WOULD YOU ADVISE A HUMAN ABOUT THE PROCESS OF DYING?
The importance of preparation is essential. It is a test that you cannot prepare too much for ahead of time. Forgive ahead of time. Deathbed confessions are a frequent need.

Confess ahead of time. Gifts and wills are put together for the end. Give gifts and love ahead of time. Give all of yourself ahead of time. Words and wishes are often kept until later. Give love now before it is too late.

THANK YOU FOR THE WISDOM. YOU HAD MANY FOLLOWERS. WHAT WOULD YOU SHARE WITH THEM?
It is never too early and it is never too late. If you have something to give or share, do that now. All humans are going to leave their bodies someday. Prepare. I was a teacher. That was my way in life. The best students prepared for the test long before the time of the test. They studied with an eye on the eventual test. They learned over time for the eventual test. Students study. All know that there will be a final test. Avoiding does not help. The test will happen – prepare for it!

HOW SHOULD A STUDENT PREPARE FOR THE FINAL TEST?
Go more deeply into who you are. You are wonderfully made and greatly loved. Know this more than the facts about the human world. All is passing away. Your spirit is eternal. Get to know and love your spirit. Prayer is good – meditation is better. Meditation is good – contemplation is better. Contemplation is good – love is better.

If you could see your spirit you would be instantly in love. It is within you. Find that jewel that is within, and you will be so in love that you will want to be there with the object of your love. Go deeper – your spirit is within you. That is what lives on after the body dies. Make friends with your spirit while you live, and you will live on in love in your spirit after dying.

IS THERE ANYTHING ELSE THAT YOU WANT TO TEACH US?

Part Three: People Prepared to Die

Naturally it would be about love. Love is how we were formed. Love is our essence. Invest in love; learn the ways of love and you will love your living and your dying. Many enjoy a peaceful death. Learn that art. Learn to love and dying will be easy.

CONTEMPLATION (Mother Teresa)
"I would not come back as who I had been," she says. This may seem strange to you. Do you believe there is a coming back for some people? If so, surely this is unlikely for someone so full of love and devotion, who served others all of her life? We wonder: who is she now and what is she doing in the afterlife? We should expect a "dramatic change" and a "deeper essence" she tells us. The Bible says that when we honor and develop our in-dwelling spirit we receive these fruits: "joy, peace, patience, kindness, goodness, faithfulness, gentleness, and self-control." In what ways have these fruits been given to you during your lifetime? Which of these fruits do you want to work on as you prepare for your dying? Write them down.

_____
_____
_____
_____
_____

When Mother Teresa made a trip to an African region suffering drought and starvation, a reporter asked her: But why did you come when you know you cannot possibly be successful here? I didn't come to be successful; I came to be faithful, she answered. In what ways have you been faithful to the God of your understanding and those you love?

_____
_____
_____
_____
_____

The purpose of Mother Teresa's living and dying was to trust in the Lord and give love to those around her. Love, she says, is a gift. What is the greatest gift you have received in your life? What is the greatest gift you have given others in your life? Write them down.

_____
_____
_____
_____
_____

Love, she says, requires action. Communion, meditation, contemplation are all purposeful rituals that enrich our spirit and relationship with God and others. Sometimes taking action is as easy as gazing into the eyes of another, receiving and honoring their truth with a smile. Sometimes it is very hard but we can ask God to help us heal our relationships. Sometimes we are deeply angry at God and others. We must acknowledge these emotions and ask for what we need in order to let these feelings go. It is never too late to do this. Start now.

> **Now we see but a poor reflection as in a mirror; then we shall see face to face. Now I know in part; then I shall know fully, even as I am fully known. And now these three remain: faith, hope and love, but the greatest of these is love.**
>
> — 1 Corinthians 12:12-13

Part Three: People Prepared to Die

Long Life Writer

The writer of many books of the Bible is referred to simply as John. His books stand out for their unique view of the life of the Messiah. This man was as well prepared to die as anyone as a result of his living as the favorite of our Lord in a personal relationship.

I INVITE JOHN OF PATMOS TO TELL OF HIS DYING
I truly am the one who lived long and was blessed to see many things in a long life. I wrote mostly at the end of my life of the things that I had seen. I was the younger of those who walked with our Lord and lived the longest. I was meant to live long and write. At the end of my life, I saw many visions. I had the connection to our Lord and could interpret those revelations. I died quietly in my sleep. Because I had been taken up into spirit so many times, I moved into spirit easily.

DO YOU WANT TO SHARE ANY NEW STORIES WITH US?
Yes, I could only write so much while still in my body. As you know, writing is time consuming. When I was early in my time with our Lord, he showed me miracles about himself. It would be like the transfiguration on the mountain story. He was just with me, and he showed me his glorified body. He was so dazzlingly bright. He showed his real self to me privately. He was transcendent in his luminosity. He just shined like the sun. Later, I reflected on these personal experiences. I had seen them but I wondered about the truth of the experiences and my ability to do anything with this knowledge. I never wrote about this, but pondered it in my heart afterwards. This served as a personal inspiration to keep on writing. Writing was better than trying to tell others personally. True belief is rare.

DO YOU HAVE ANY MESSAGE FOR ME, AS YOUR SCRIBE?
Yes, keep writing even if you do not know the whole truth. Write daily and more will come through to you. Your belief will get strong with practice. It is like physical exercise. Every step in running builds the ability to run longer. Every repetition builds physical strength. The more you write, the better you will be as a writer; and the more you will believe.

I NOTICE THAT YOU USE THE WORD TRUTH OFTEN.
There is so little truth available now. All is opinion and vanity. There is undeniable truth. That is the goal. That is the goal for all. That is the goal for your writing. Write the truth for people to know about dying. The truth of dying is hidden from most people. Tell them the truth about the dying process.

WHAT IS THE TRUTH ABOUT THE DYING PROCESS?
The journey from human into spirit is spiritual. We are meant to be put into this place and taken from this world for a greater purpose. The source of all life gives and takes as it sees fit. That can be personalized or seen as logos (the Word) in action. Either way, we are meant to live and die, to be and to be taken, to live and be loved as a natural part of being human. That is the truth. It is a simple truth. Too often humans confuse their part of the play and want to determine their own experience.

THAT IS CLEAR TO ME. WHAT WOULD YOU HAVE ME DO?
Pray, meditate, fast – the simple truths of the spiritual path. The basics of the human way are eat, talk, and control. The spiritual path is just a different path. Now you need to balance the two so that you can write and leave a record of this. I did it. You can do it. This place where you are is

conducive to writing. You can create your own place for writing. In the end, I was on an island because I was considered too much for the human world. It worked out to be a blessing because it gave me a simple place to write about my experience.

THANK YOU SO MUCH.
You would do best to lighten up and simplify. This world is too full of distractions. Set up a life that is quiet and simple. Perhaps you will find your island to write on.

CONTEMPLATION (John of Patmos)
We are sent to this world to live, to love and be loved, and to die into spirit with a greater purpose, John tells us. Death is not the end but a new beginning. This good news gives us hope for the future but it does not take away all of the fears and other emotions that dying brings. How can we deal with these? John says by building up our spiritual strength. Our belief will get stronger with practice. And how do we do that. His advice is to set up a life that is quiet and simple. What will you need to change in your life in order to do this? Write down your ideas and fears about this; pray for guidance first.

_____
_____
_____
_____

Can you identify what your purpose has been so far in your life on Earth? When have you felt joy in your life? Some talk about family and work and friends. Can you identify examples of what you actually did that helped you in these relationships. What word would others use to describe your greatest gift or skill?

_____
_____
_____
_____

John's greatest gift was writing to tell others about God and Jesus. It was not a popular topic for many at that time. He had been banished to the Island of Patmos, which turned out to be exactly the right place for him to write. When have changes in your life turned out to have hidden blessings like this?

___

As humans John says our focus is to eat, talk, and control. When we are in spirit, our focus is to pray, meditate, and fast. While here we need to balance all of these. What happens when you are out of balance? For example, when you are trying so hard to control someone or something that all else doesn't seem to matter? What happens when you let go of control and let God be in charge of your life? Write down examples.

___

It is often difficult for humans to face reality; we are good at denial and delusion. This keeps us in false control and out of spirit. John writes that the truth will set us free. Make a list of what makes up your current, undeniable reality. Compose a prayer that acknowledges that reality and asks the God of your understanding for clarity and wisdom to face your truths and your dying.

___

"Hope is the thing with feathers that perches in the soul and sings the tune without the words and never stops at all."

— Emily Dickinson, 1830-1886

His Plan Fulfilled

Ya Shua lived in a time that was very different from now. He let the flower of his life unfold over time. He let go of this earth as his particular plan of dying unfolded as a service to others.

I INVITE YA SHUA OF JUDEA IN THIS DAY. DO YOU WANT TO TELL OF YOUR DYING?
It was proscribed well in advance. My dying started before my living. My way was set out as surely as the path of the stars. I was aware of what my dying would be like well ahead of time. I tried to tell all about how I was going to die in Jerusalem, but few had ears to hear. My mother knew.

WHAT WAS IT LIKE FOR YOU TO NOT BE UNDERSTOOD?
It was a source of sadness. I wept often. The people could not understand the larger picture of the plan of God. I talked about tradition. I talked about the Torah. People were mostly caught up in their own way of thinking. Now and then I could get through to people. Their faith was the most important variable to what they understood. Spiritual matters are largely a matter of faith.

WHAT WOULD YOU WANT TO SHARE?
My life and death were set out ahead of time. There was very little choice. God had called me to a particular path. The only variable was my will as to whether or not I would follow the path. All lives are like my life. Life is set out ahead of time. Literally, before time occurs we are destined for a certain path. Humans have the ability to follow through on the plan or not. It is simple. It is not easy to stay on the path.

Part Three: People Prepared to Die

DO YOU HAVE ANY ADVICE FOR US HUMANS?
Just like my dying was proscribed, so are all deaths proscribed. Humans have the ability to agree or not. The main way to follow the path is to go deep within and hear the ways of the path for the individual. I often went away to pray and stay attuned to the plan that was imprinted on my soul. It was all within the entire time of my life on earth. It unfolded like a flower over time and I kept track as the plan unfolded. When I was alive in Judea, this was a common way of knowing life. Now, it is a distant way of knowing. Humans are meant to listen for the plan of the spirit within them. Their peace and quiet is essential for the unfolding of the flower. The spirit is like a beautiful flower within. The essence of a jewel within is also appropriate.

HOW DO WE CONNECT WITH THIS INNER SPIRIT?
Silence is best. Silence is not available to everyone. The will is most important for how the individual connects with their inner plan. The will to find the path is most important for finding of the path. You found your way in silence at the Merton monastery. Other people find the inner path in different ways. Prayer helps. Love is the best path.

HOW DO WE BEST LOVE?
As the human is set up to love – that type of love is best. My path was service to others. I healed others who wanted healing. I washed the feet of others who wanted washing. I died on the cross as service to others.

HOW WAS YOUR DYING ON THE CROSS?
You may not be able to write down English words that could tell the story well. It was shame beyond description.

Crucifixion is the most shameful of human dying ways. I was naked before everyone. I was beaten and bloodied in full view of my family and friends. I was put to death by those who I was sent to serve. The physical pain was extreme, and the shame was greater. My dying was the antidote for the pride of humanity. I took on shame to serve those who were slaves to their pride. God so loved the world that I was sent to become shame for the healing of the pride of man. I willingly followed the plan and took on shame in dying for the healing of humanity.

THANK YOU. DO YOU HAVE ANY LAST MESSAGES TO US? Keep your eyes on the prize of eternal life. There, lives are short and shallow by nature. Transcend these narrow lives and look toward the greater life of spirit. Looking up to the stars of the universe would be a good way to encourage all to look beyond their own small lives. There is a human life to be lived, and there is a greater life to be lived in spirit. Focus on the greater life. A clear focus on the spiritual path will make the dying process peaceful for humans as they pass into spirit.

Part Three: People Prepared to Die

CONTEMPLATION (Ya Shua of Judea)
To understand what God's plan for us is we must go deep within, he says. We must seek quiet and peace and pray. Have you ever been on a silent retreat? There are many retreat centers that offer these, but you can make your own retreat to nature or to a holy sanctuary in your church, synagogue, mosque, or chapel. While prayer helps, love is also essential. In what ways do you love the God of your understanding? In what ways do you demonstrate your faith?

_____
_____
_____
_____
_____

We also need willingness to follow God's spiritual plan for us. We have to learn to give up self-will for God's will and turn toward accepting suggestions, shouldering our responsibilities, and taking risks to change and grow as needed to meet God's plan. We must cultivate humility. None of this is very easy to do. Remember to tell yourself you are a child of God, and God's grace is sufficient for you to choose the right path. At this point in your life, what do you think your spiritual path is calling you to do? What is the next right thing for you to do?

_____
_____
_____
_____
_____

Eternal life often seems very far away, but as we have learned from the spirits' messages, heaven is just a heartbeat away.

Can you draw a picture of what your heaven might look like? Can you use your faith to understand what lies ahead for you?

> **"Now faith is being sure of what we hope for and certain of what we do not see."**
>
> — Hebrews 11:1

Part Four: Conclusion

Summary and Acknowledgements

Hopefully, this workbook has been helpful for your living and your future dying. This book started out as an academic research paper and has progressed to this fresh view of how we humans go through the healing process called dying.

Yes, this process of dying is healing when done well. Our best ally is a consistent commitment to the process of preparing to die with a purpose. Our dying, like our living, goes best when we are intentional and consistent in our actions.

Your dying will be unique to you. Your dying process could already be starting. If you have gotten through this workbook, it is a sure sign that something is moving in your life. We encourage you to make this moving as best as you can. Toward that end, we honor the lives of the twenty-one messengers who have served as examples for us all:

Abby, we thank you for recovering quickly from a surprise death and starting this process of writing about all who survive and thrive after death.

Lily, we thank you for being a shining star that blazed briefly in this life before passing on to more life ahead.

Abraham Lincoln, we thank you for caring about us so much that you gave your life, then and today, for our well-being.

Martin Luther King, Jr., we thank you for accepting the way of the martyr as the way of a warrior for justice in the world.

John Kennedy, we thank you for enduring the most famous of deaths in an honorable way.

Robert Kennedy, we thank you for never giving up or giving in when it was dark or difficult.

John Lennon, we thank you for leading us in new ways that lifted our hearts and spirits.

Bill, my young friend, we thank you for your gift of friendship as you showed the way of joy in dying young.

Dave, we thank you for being the good brother who was always there to help in times of joy and sorrow.

Carol, we thank you for being such a bright light in our lives and sharing your warmth and love with us.

Robin Williams, we thank you for bringing joy to our hearts as you showed us the way of laughter and pain.

Jacklyn Kennedy, we thank you for holding up the highest standards in living and dying.

Thomas Merton, we thank you for telling your story so well and inspiring us to tell our story.

Dr. Raymond Brown, we thank you for writing so clearly about the death and dying of our Messiah.

Aunt M, we thank you for your healing touch as you ministered to patients and the boy.

Grandma Ellen, we thank you for all your light and grace on the path of living and dying.

Dr. Elizabeth Kubler-Ross, we thank you for opening new doors for us to move into new views of death and dying.

George Harrison, we thank you for showing us how to move from the human to the spiritual.

Mother Teresa, we thank you for taking the simple path to teach us to love.

Part Four: Conclusion

John of Patmos, we thank you for always being faithful and for writing of your love.

Ya Shua, our undying gratitude to you for always saying yes for us.

Guided Meditation
Repeat this meditation often as you prepare for your dying.

Find a quiet place with a comfortable chair where you will not be disturbed. Rest a while and relax your body and pray for openness to receive whatever comes to you during this time. Focus your attention on your breathing, letting any thoughts pass through your mind. Close your eyes and notice how air enters your nostrils. Continue letting all thoughts go and slowly bring your attention back to your breathing for at least five minutes.

Now think of your spirit as a white dove with shimmering feathers. This dove can fly wherever your spirit tells it. Your spirit is totally and joyfully at ease. You have no fears and few emotions even though you have memory of being in your body on Earth. Wherever your spirit leads, your dove goes willingly and happily and without fear.

In an instant you are aware of what your new purpose is in spirit. Your new purpose may be related to your interests in life on Earth. Or it may be a totally new interest. It may be something you wished you could explore on Earth but circumstances kept you from doing so. As your spirit soars in pursuit of your new purpose, notice how your body feels. Are your muscles tight or relaxed? Is your breathing slow and steady or rapid and strained? Ask your spirit to reveal something about your interests and experiences in the next world. Be open to listening to any answers that come.

Rest your spirit. Your beautiful white dove is now sitting peacefully on a tree branch. When you are totally relaxed and open, begin imagining what your dying might be like on Earth. Remember that when you are in spirit you are protected from the strong emotions you felt while in your body. You are literally as light as a feather. What did your dying body feel on Earth? Was someone there with you or

Part Four: Conclusion

were you alone? Were you able to say your goodbyes? Did you have time to prepare for your death? Was your passing into spirit an easy one? Notice how you can feel empathy for your body and who you were on Earth, but you no longer feel the emotions and physical symptoms of your dying. You have begun a new life that is hugely different and more beautiful than your mind could ever have imagined. This brings you great joy. Rest in this joy for a while, then when you are ready return to your body feeling refreshed and free.

The Impact of Spiritual Beliefs During Times of Personal Crisis

When we face dying, loss, and grief most of us are challenged to review our spiritual beliefs. What do we believe about how the world works; about God's relationship with our world; about the role God does or doesn't play in death and dying, loss and life? We search for comfort and personal truth. Answer the following questions (provided by Rev. Michael Jemmott) to help identify and reflect on some of your beliefs. **I believe that:**

    Dying starts when the doctor says so. _____
    Death can be premature. _____
    Death is OK in old age. _____
    Parents die before children. _____
    Young people should not die. _____
    It is God's will when death occurs. _____
    Dying is a form of punishment. _____
    Death can be defeated with a good fight. _____
    God takes people by causing their death. _____
    Living is the highest good. _____

There are no right or wrong answers; there are only your answers! Give yourself time to reflect on why you believe what you believe. Give yourself permission to strengthen or change your beliefs as the Spirit moves and works within you. If you find you cannot believe in God right now, can you believe in a power greater than yourself?

Religion is one way we practice what we believe. Do you have one? Do you know what your expectations are for support from your religious community during times of crisis? If you feel you are not getting the support you need from your religious community, is there someone you can talk to about this? If you currently do not have a religious community, are there other ways you find spiritual connection and support in your life?

When we are having a physical crisis, we seek medical help. Similarly, when we are having a spiritual crisis we can take action. We can ask for help from God and from other spiritual seekers.

References

Abbott, James; Rice, Elaine. 1997. **Designing Camelot: The Kennedy White House Restoration**. John Wiley and Sons, New York.

Arrien, Angeles, 2013. **The Four-Fold Way: Walking the Paths of the Warrior, Teacher, Healer, and Visionary.** Harper Collins, New York.

Becker, Verne. (Ed.), 1993. **Recovery Devotional Bible: New International Version.** Zondervan Publishing, Grand Rapids, Michigan

Brown, David. **Rolling Stone,** Issue 1217, September 11, 2014, "Robin Williams, 1951-2014."

Brown, Raymond E**.**, 1994. **The Death of the Messiah: From Gethsemane to the Grave.** Doubleday, New York.

Davis, Saskia. "Signs and Symptoms of Inner Peace." Copyright 1984. www.symptomsofinnerpeace.net.

Frankl, Viktor. **Man's Search for Meaning**. 1946/2004. Rider Books, London.

Guggenheim, Bill & Judy. **1996. Hello From Heaven.** Bantam, New York.

Kubler-Ross, Elizabeth, 2011. **On Death and Dying: What the Dying Have to Teach Doctors, Nurses, Clergy, and their own Families**. Scribner, New York.

Annotated Bibliography

Anderson, George and Barone, Andrew. 2001. *Walking in the Garden of Souls: George Anderson's Advice from the Hereafter, for Living in the Here and Now.* Berkley Books, New York.

    George Anderson "has a unique awareness of what… departed souls want us to know: To reassure us of a life beyond our physical one on Earth. To teach us how to live better now in preparation for the hereafter. To let us know that they are waiting for us.

Aquinas, Thomas. *Summa Theologica.* 2014. Catholic Way Publishing, London, England.

    This most rigorous of all theological treatises approaches the issues of death and life from logical and theological perspectives. Though this 800 year old work is not easy reading, it does lay the scholastic foundation for a rational philosophy of the process of thinking about deeper issues. The central concept that Aquinas adds to the discussion is the highly intentional nature of the process of the will in the literature that addresses issues of human action. The *Summa* provides a compendium of ideas covering thousands of years in this sweeping work that provides philosophical and theological strength to the case for an intentional death.

Brown, Raymond. *The Death of the Messiah: From Gethsemane to the Grave.* 1994. Doubleday, New York.

    This seminal work of Scriptural commentary presents the account of the intentional death of Jesus of Nazareth. It includes the text that describes the main biblical narrative of the passion and dying process in the life of the Messiah. Each of the four Gospels presents this story as the longest continuous narrative in describing the life of the Messiah. This account of dying holds great weight in western culture.

Byock, Ira. *Dying Well.* 1998. Riverhead Books, Riverhead, NY.
This best-selling book by a practicing physician presents the process of dying well from a medical point of view. The chief idea presented is that of entertaining the prospect of growth at the end of life. Though Dr. Byock entertains some theological values, the author stresses the potential for human growth in the tragedy of dying. This highly successful book presents a widely held philosophical approach in the technological milieu of Western culture.

Davies, Douglas. *The Theology of Death.* 2008. Bloomsbury T & T Clark, New York.
This book presents a contemporary theology for the Christian mystery of death.
Davies presents a theology that is a process of inquiry and reflection rather than a set of answers to a question. This theology is the opposite of abstract concepts that formal theology usually are concerned with in their presentations. For such an imposing title, the book is actually a lively resource for Christians that seek a meaningful approach to a central idea in the life of the faithful.

Devers, Edie. *Goodbye Again: Experiences with Departed Loved Ones.* 1997. Andrews and McMeel Books, Kansas City, MO.
This book contains examples of "After-Death Communication (ADC): a phenomenon whereby survivors

report having contact with loved ones who have died. This contact may come through a strong sense of presence, a vivid dream, or through one of the five senses, such as seeing the deceased sitting in a favorite chair or smelling her perfume.

Ellens, J. Harold. *Radical Grace: How Belief in a Benevolent God Benefits Our Health.* 2007. Praeger, Westport, CT.
　　This book emphasizes the belief in a benevolent God who benefits human health. It also emphasizes scriptural efficiency as it also presents a psychology of healing. The result is a fascinating account of psycho-theology that benefits the human person. The author employs an eclectic combination of sources that lead toward a radical approach to grace for the healing process in humans.

Graham, Billy. *Facing Death and the Life After.* 1987. WPub Group, NY.
　　This book from a widely known Christian author is included because of the theological nature of his approach to confronting death. Graham's human approach to the Christian concept of death, emphasizes the role of the individual in the intentional process of dying. This unique approach to dying will appeal to a sector of Western Christians who emphasize the positive action of the individual.

Halifax, Joan. *Being with Dying: Cultivating Compassion and Fearlessness in the Presence of Death.* 2008. Shambhala. Boston, CT.
　　Inspired by traditional Buddhist teachings, Halifax offers lessons from dying people and caregivers, as well as guided meditations to help readers contemplate death

without fear, develop a commitment to helping others, and transform suffering and resistance into courage.

Heidegger, Martin. *Being and Time.* 2013. Amazon Digital Services, Inc.
No serious literary review of life and death could ignore a book that, though acclaimed by many, is largely considered too abstract to be of use. And yet, it is the deep philosophical nature of Heidegger's work that moves it into being included in a review of literature for approaching an intentional death. Though, "being into death", may not be a popular idea in the popular culture, it carries relevance in the dialogue of dying.

Hicks, Esther and Jerry. *The Amazing Power of Deliberate Intent: Living the Art of Allowing.* 2006. Hay House/ Balboa Press, Bloomington, IN.
This book pushes the edge of healing and intentional dying with another set of sources concerning the healing power of spirit. Death is strongly presented as a new beginning in the experience of the human person. These authors present a contemporary approach to the spiritual issues involved in the dying and healing process. Though this type of book may not be for all, it is another contemporary look at the Western consciousness in the area of dying and health.

Hogan, R. Craig and Gary E. Schwartz. *Afterlife Communication: 16 Proven Methods; 85 True Accounts.* 2014. Greater Reality Publications. Greaterreality.com.
This book contains descriptions of methods people are using today to communicate with loved ones who have passed away. The authors are acknowledged

experts in afterlife communications who developed the methods, are using them, and are teaching people how to use them. The book contains actual accounts of people's connections with their loved ones on the other side using these methods.

Kubler-Ross, Elizabeth. *On Death and Dying: What the Dying Have to Teach Doctors, Nurses, Clergy, and Their Own Families.* 2011, Scribner, New York.

This book from a physician has become part of our collective consciousness regarding the subject of death. The five stages have been adopted by many parts of Western healing as key human concepts. And yet, to read this book, is to appreciate anew the ground breaking wisdom that brought this compassionate physician to state the obvious. Any Western analysis of the issue of intentional dying, and its related wellness, needs to include this seminal work in its discussion. The groundbreaking approach that was articulated in this book has now passed into our collective subconscious as individuals and patients.

Kubler-Ross, Elizabeth. *To Live Until We Say Goodbye.* 1978/1980. Fireside, Whitby, Ontario, Canada.

This follow up book shows the growth of this pioneer in the genre of intentional dying. Her sensitivity to the dying process discloses itself in her growth from a philosophical approach to death and dying to a higher appreciation of the process that all humans encounter from a higher perspective. Though the physician encountered some criticism in her more developed approaches to dying, her work provided an enhanced perspective from which to view this issue. Her deep appreciation of the role of the individual continues to serve as a beacon for those who serve those in transition.

Langs, Robert. *Beyond Yahweh and Jesus: Bringing Death's Wisdom to Faith, Spirituality, and Psychoanalysis.* 2013. Jason Aronson, Inc., New York.
This book presents a compelling account of the interplay between death, faith, spirituality, and psychoanalysis. The central theme of human anxiety concerning death and dying is taken on in a broad approach to the synergy between seeming disparate disciplines. The author presents a compelling approach to combining the intentional death of Jesus Christ and the lessening of psychological anxiety regarding the seemingly predatory nature of death.

Moody, Raymond. *Life after Life.* 1975/2001. HarperOne, New York.
This seminal work by a physician has proved to be the first of the largest selling set of books in contemporary Western culture concerning the issue of dying. Popular culture has embraced this set of ideas concerning the experiences of patients in the dying process in hospitals. Though the author is a physician, in addition to being a Doctor of Philosophy, these ideas remain on the fringes of contemporary medical practice. This book is presented as a resource for the implementation of a process with patients in the present milieu.

Moll, Robert and Winner, Lauren. *The Art of Dying: Living Fully Into the Life to Come.* 2013. InterVarsity Books, Nottingham, England.
This book presents a theological model for living fully into the life to come. Moll seems especially sensitive to the concept of dying gradually over time. Moll also

presents a well-researched account of the process of dying well through Christian rituals and disciplines. Moll presents a spirituality of dying that is both realistic and practical in its approach to working with people in the process of the art of dying.

Morse, Melvin. *Closer to the Light: Learning From the Near-Death Experiences of Children.* 1990. Ivy Books, New York.

In hundreds of interviews with children who had once been declared clinically dead, a leading pediatrician found the same description, the same experience, the same attitude, over and over again: that the end of life is serene and joyful, a welcome event not to be feared.

Muller, Wayne. *Sabbath: Finding Rest, Renewal, and Delight in Our Busy Lives.* 2013. Bantam, New York.

This book presents a spiritual perspective for a sacred rhythm of living intentionally in times of rest. This spiritual work by Muller advocates for the use of the ancient practice of intentionally resting into problematic life issues. This challenging book presents yet another creative approach to working through the process of living through life and death processes for humans who have a faith perspective.

Neal, Mary C. *To Heaven and Back: A Doctor's Extraordinary Account of Her Death, Heaven, Angels, and Life Again.* 2011. Waterbrook Press. Colorado Springs, CO.

Dr. Neal drowned in a kayak accident. She moved from death to eternal life and back again. This book will "reacquaint you with the hope, wonder, and promise of heaven, while enriching your own faith and walk with God."

Nicklas, Tobias, & Hieke, Thomas. *The Day of Atonement.*
 This contemporary book presents a compelling presentation for the ancient practice of atonement. This book presents numerous accounts of the practices and liturgies of humans who seek reconciliation with the divine. These texts present the case for the process of reconciliation between the divine and the human. The complex and mysterious ways of antiquity serve as compelling inspiration for the practice of human activity in search of union with the divine.

Nouwen, Henri. *Finding My Way Home.* 2004. The Crossroad Publishing Company.
 This book describes a spiritual death. Nouwen is able to bridge the theological issues and the human concerns in the process of dying. This book provides a theoretical balance between the theological and the human. Though the writer is a Catholic priest, the text provides a compelling presentation of the death well lived. In some ways this book serves as the fulcrum for the movement from the religious and spiritual to the more human issues in the process of living and dying.

O'Rourke, Michelle. *Befriending Death: Henri Nouwen and a Spirituality of Dying.* 2009. Orbis Books, Mary Knell, NY.
 This contemporary book is an appropriate contrast to the previous book about approaches to dying. This author presents a kinder view of the process of dying, that while being spiritual in nature, is more friendly in literary tone. O'Rourke presents chapters on dying well and caring well as a reflection on the death of Henri Nouwen.

Piper, Don. 90 Minutes in Heaven. 2004. Baker Publishing Group, Grand Rapids, MI.
   This book offers a glimpse into a very real dimension of God's reality. It encourages those recovering from serious injuries and those dealing with the loss of a loved one.

Rahner, Karl. *On the Theology of Death.* 1961. Herder and Herder, New York.
   This book presents death as an integral event in the life of humans. Rahner is concerned with opening up new points of view in the traditional view of death. The central thesis of this work is the need for openness in the theological view of death from a Christian perspective. One chapter focuses on the Christian death as an intentional death with Christ. Though it is not easy reading, this book provides depth and weight to the concept of human involvement in the process of dying.

Ramsey, Paul. *The Patient as Person. (2nd Ed.).* 2002. Yale University Press, London, England.
   This book serves as an enlightened approach to the issues of medical ethics in the field of death and dying. This author makes a strong case for the proper respect for the treatment of patients in a medical care setting.

Solomon, Lewis D. and Epperly, Bruce F. *Walking in the Light.* 2004. Christian Board of Publication, St. Louis, MO.
   This book is a vision of healing and wholeness for the patient. The presentation supports the concepts and wellness from a spiritual point of view. The author

combines Jewish-Christian practices with human approaches to the healing for the whole person. This book makes the transition into more alternative approaches to the process of intentional healing and dying.

Warren, Richard. *The Purpose Driven Life.* 2012. Zondervan, Grand Rapids, MI.

This best- selling book by a Christian author presents the way of living with an intentional approach to planning major life events. A central idea for Warren is that life events are to be based on eternal theological principles rather than contemporary cultural values. This book relies heavily on Christian scripture for its approach to life issues. The chief value of this book in this literature review is the idea of the intentional nature of all life events. This approach would apply to that most private of all decisions, the decision to be integrally involved in the dying and healing processes. Purpose driven living implies purpose driven involvement in all areas of living and dying.

About the Authors

John Michael Ketzer has been serving the dying since meeting Mother Teresa in 1994. Since that time he has journeyed with hundreds of individuals through the dying process. These twenty years of work have provided wisdom to share with others. During 2014 John began working with Abby (see Part One) with a desire to be of help to her grieving parents. Abby's responses to John's prayers and meditation resulted in the process used to contact other spirits and the desire to pass along their wisdom to others. John is currently a Chaplain at Santa Rosa Memorial Hospital in Santa Rosa, California.

As a psychotherapist, Kay Talbot, Ph.D. has worked with many individuals, families and groups experiencing loss and life transitions. She is the author of <u>What Forever Means After the Death of a Child: Transcending the Trauma; Living With the Loss, 2002, Taylor & Francis, New York.</u> Her ground-breaking research on the death of an only child has been published in <u>The Hospice Journal</u> and <u>Omega, Journal of Death and Dying.</u> Dr. Talbot has also authored Carenotes published by Abby Press on the topics of dying well and dealing with grief, anger, and depression. She lives in Vallejo, California.

Made in the USA
Middletown, DE
18 October 2024

62846351R00102